"I've always appreciated A. J. Juliani's blog, and this book is similarly filled with practical, classroom-tested advice for PBL teachers. He makes a persuasive case for PBL and, even better, offers lots of tools and wisdom to guide teachers in creating and facilitating high-quality PBL units. Also great to see are the many examples of actual teachers and projects."

— **John Larmer,** Editor-in-Chief, Buck Institute for Education

"*The PBL Playbook* is a must-read book if you are looking to meet the needs of all learners—now and in their future. A. J. Juliani not only provides a compelling argument for why it is critical that we empower students and create authentic learning experiences through Project-Based Learning; he provides the strategies and examples for how to make that vision a reality in any context."

— **Katie Martin,** Head of Partnerships-West, AltSchool and Author of *Learner-Centered Innovation*

"*The PBL Playbook* is an inspirational and accessible guide to project-based learning. A. J. Juliani lays out a clear blueprint, addressing the burning questions teachers have as they take the PBL leap forward. It's packed full of concrete examples and comprehensive sample projects you can use tomorrow!"

— **John Spencer,** Professor, Author of *LAUNCH* and *Empower*

THE PBL PLAYBOOK

A. J. JULIANI

THE PBL PLAYBOOK

A Step-by-Step Guide to Actually Doing **Project-Based Learning**

Write Nerdy Publishing

First Printing, 2018

ISBN-13: 978-0-692-14490-9

Printed in the United States of America

This book is dedicated to

the 47 teachers who shared their PBL stories in this book,
and the countless other teachers, coaches, and leaders
who have transformed learning for their students with PBL.
To the lone nuts, first followers, and trailblazers
making a difference in classrooms around the world,
I say thank you and keep pushing all of us.
Remember, you're just one project away . . .

Contents

Part 3: Becoming a PBL Designer—Taking Action to Create

Foreword

XOXXOXOOXO

Have you ever poured your heart and soul into an idea, obsessing over the details, only to find yourself exhausted as your idea results in a flop? Of course you have. As any experienced teacher will tell you, great learning is a product of trial and error. The key to survival is recognizing you are not alone, learning from your mistakes, and calling upon the lessons learned by those around you.

Throughout each (American) football season, millions of viewers spend hours glued to their screens watching athletes enact carefully rehearsed moves against equally prepared (most of the time) opponents. These professional athletes lean on their years of experience, the advice of their coaches, and, of course, a meticulously crafted playbook. As a classroom teacher or district administrator, we know you would love to have access to this kind comprehensive resource. The *PBL Playbook* draws on A.J. Juliani's years as a teacher, coach, and administrator to offer a multidimensional approach to implementing project based learning (PBL).

In the last five years, A.J. has tackled challenges surrounding student-centered learning by offering educators guides that encompass such topics as Genius Hour and design thinking. While writing *Hacking Project Based Learning*, we drew upon his work and inspiration to provide insight into PBL. Now he broadens his lens by tackling project based learning from multiple angles, which notably include: why PBL is a non-negotiable in today's classrooms, how to gradually hand over the learning process to students, a five-step system for planning projects, and countless authentic examples from those doing the work *right now*.

And, of course, *now* is the time to start implementing PBL or to take your PBL work even further. Countless studies tell us the longer students are in school, the less they buy in to what they're doing in our classrooms. Engagement for educators doesn't necessarily equate to relevance for students. And, according to Anthony Salcito, Microsoft VP of Education, "Our students are learning without us." As a result, so many educators have been left scrambling for a silver bullet that'll set everything straight. While we don't think such a silver bullet exists, when it comes to instructional approaches we believe project based learning is as close as we're going to get. When thoughtfully designed, PBL experiences immerse *students* in inquiry, maximize *student* voice and choice, and meet *students* where they are (as opposed to educators forcing students to conform). Also, in a profession in which initiative fatigue has become as common as bored students taking the long way to the bathroom, PBL is truly an approach (and mindset) that encompasses and provides context for so many hard hitting practices: creating a culture of inquiry, crafting essential questions, providing feedback, assessment literacy, student reflection, and more.

Whether you are a novice looking for a place to start, or a PBL veteran looking for a fresh approach, the *PBL Playbook* is sure to be the guide that will help you and your students along the way.

We wish you the best of luck of luck on your PBL journey!

Ross Cooper
@RossCoops31

Erin Murphy
@MurphysMusings5

INTRODUCTION:

From Tickets to Learning

XOXXOXOOXO

It was toward the middle of my first year teaching (eighth grade) when it hit me: my class was spinning out of control, and it was all my fault.

I was an eager first-year teacher, with an awesome mentor who taught language arts with me in the same middle school team. My students were busy writing papers, doing cool projects that we came up with, and reading in literature circles. I was also lucky to have a lot of technology in the classroom early in my career. It was a really good spot to start teaching, and I was messing it all up.

You see, when my students started to bring their homework in late (or not at all) toward the end of the first marking period, and when our class discussions around a rather boring novel took a downward spiral to the "quiet zone" (I was good at wait time, but not that good!)—I tried to problem-solve the issue.

Instead of asking my colleagues what they might do, I thought I had the perfect remedy to fix the situation (in reality this was my biggest mistake).

I went to the local teacher store (Becker's) and bought up a whole roll of tickets. Yes, those tickets.

I came back to school the next week and told my students all about our new "rewards" program for our class. It was way too complicated and included "roll over" tickets that could be used as extra credit points for their end of the marking period grade . . . I know, a bit ridiculous.

Still, in the beginning, it worked.

Students were more attentive during our class discussions, offering up opinions and trying to talk as much as possible. Homework was turned in on time more frequently, and the kids were excited to come to class with a chance to earn some extra tickets!

During the second marking period, things began to unravel. I handed out a new assignment about a nonfiction book we were reading.

The first question from my students was "Is there a way to get extra tickets for reading the book faster?"

The second question was "Mr. J, when can we get tickets with this activity?"

And so on, for the next ten minutes . . . all about tickets.

Then at the close of the second marking period, things started to be really interesting (or out of control depending on your perspective).

Kids were trading tickets with each other. I'm pretty sure I saw a "ticket deal" go down in the hallway where money might have been exchanged for tickets.

It was a free-for-all. I had messed up big time.

But I kept digging a bigger hole.

At the start of the third marking period I told my students that tickets were not going to be used for grades any more. That they could only be used for "whole class" activities like a pizza party.

Most of my students complained, but I stuck to my guns, and we moved forward with the new "tickets for pizza" program in Mr. J's class.

I had set an arbitrary number of 100 tickets.

Now, every day in class, students would ask why they didn't get a ticket for participating, or for handing something in early, or for doing something above and beyond.

I wilted under the pressure and started handing them out more frequently, thinking that at least it was just for pizza, and not for grades.

When we finally got to have the pizza party (a short three weeks later), I was exhausted. I told my students we were going to take a ticket break.

And consequently, they revolted.

Homework started to come in late, class discussions went back to a whole lot of wait time, and I even received a few parent e-mails asking why I had stopped the tickets because their son/daughter was really motivated and now had nothing to look forward to (ouch!).

I had realized (the extremely hard way) that tickets, pizza parties, and other rewards did not work in my classroom. It was a humbling and embarrassing situation. And one that I completely brought upon myself.

If Tickets Don't Work, Then What Does Work?

"What rewards and punishments do is induce compliance, and this they do very well indeed. If your objective is to get people to obey an order, to show up on time and do what they're told, then bribing or threatening them may be sensible strategies. But if your objective is to get long-term quality in the workplace, to help students become careful thinkers and self-directed learners, or to support children in developing good values, then rewards, like punishments, are absolutely useless. In fact, as we are beginning to see, they are worse than useless—they are actually counterproductive."

-Alfie Kohn, *Punished by Rewards: The Trouble with Gold Stars, Incentive Plans, A's, Praise, and Other Bribes*

I was pointed in the direction of Alfie Kohn's work when I told a colleague about my ticket debacle. Honestly, they never taught us any of this stuff (what motivates learners) in college, and teaching is a trial-by-fire type of job.

When I reflect back on my first year teaching, this lesson was by far the most important one I learned, and the subsequent reading I did about motivation and engagement helped me to do things way differently in my class than I ever would have if I didn't have the ticket disaster.

In Jonathan C. Erwin's book *The Classroom of Choice*, he opens up by discussing the myths around rewards in education, and what the research actually says:

> *Actually, contrary to conventional wisdom, rewards are no more effective in motivating students than threats and punishment. In his book* Punished by Rewards, *Alfie Kohn (1993) examines*

the research on external incentives and concludes that the "do this and you'll get that" approach to motivation fails. Citing hundreds of studies, Kohn discusses the reasons that incentives such as stickers, pizza parties, free time, trips to the toy barrel, and even As do not work. The most important reason for teachers may be that "rewards change the way people feel about what they do."

He explains that when a student hears "If you do this, then you'll get that," the message to the learner is "There must be something wrong with this if you have to give me that to get me to do it."

Thus, what we are doing when we offer a reward for learning or following classroom rules, whether we realize it or not, is "killing off the interest in the very thing we are bribing them to do." Jensen echoes Kohn's concerns regarding rewards, warning that "students will want [rewards] each time the behavior is required; they'll want an increasingly valuable reward . . . [and that] the use of rewards actually damages intrinsic motivation."[1]

When I dug into the many studies Kohn references in his book, an emerging theme kept rising to the surface:

"All rewards have the same effect. They dilute the pure joy that comes from success itself."

Erwin points out the work of Eric Jensen in his book *Teaching with the Brain in Mind*, who echoes Kohn's concerns regarding rewards, warning that "students will want [rewards] each time the behavior is required; they'll want an increasingly valuable reward . . . [and that] the use of rewards actually damages intrinsic motivation."[2]

There is one simple change I made as a teacher (and a change many teachers have made around the globe) that provides more opportunity for motivation, engagement, and empowerment than anything else I've seen.

I started to give my students choice in the learning.

Choice, it turns out, is an incredibly easy way to get kids excited about learning. Why? Well, when students have a choice, their attention is not out of necessity (you must do *this*, in order to get *that*) but instead out of interest.

Choice fuels their engagement and motivation. It fuels their learning.

Just as it still does for all of us adults. We thrive when we get to learn about something we are interested in and curious about, and we tend to go through the motions when we are forced to learn something new that we aren't particularly interested in at the moment.

But choice was only the beginning. Choice led me down a path where I was able to give my students ownership over their learning, challenging them with real-world authentic projects that create deep learning experiences.

Changing the Game of School to Focus Again on the Learning

Over the past decade, I've been frustrated and down about a lot of the traditional ways we play the "game of school" in education. Heck, there were many times I wasn't sure if innovation had a place in education.

But something interesting happened when I took action to create solutions around these problems, instead of complaining about my circumstances.

I was frustrated as a teacher a few years ago when I thought all my 11th-grade students cared about was their grades. Out of this frustration came the 20% Project in my class and a true project-based learning experience with choice, voice, and real problems to solve.

I was desperate for a new way to teach students about human rights violations and genocide. Having them read articles and watch a few videos wasn't cutting it, because the students needed to "do something" about these issues. Out of this desperation came a collaborative project that my students helped create—Project: Global Inform.

A few years ago, as a staff developer many of **our staff members were frustrated** that they had to learn about a new tool with the entire staff during an in-service when they already were using it—why have the same training when everyone was on different levels. Our game-based professional development missions came out of this frustration.

In my first role as an administrator, **a fantastic teacher I worked with was frustrated** with how "Industrial Arts" still looked, for the most part, like it did when he was in high school. After a lot of hard work, this frustration turned into a new ninth-grade course (creative design and engineering) and a reworking of the entire scope and sequence to create a true Maker Department.

Now, a group of teachers in my district were frustrated that our students weren't getting some of the same opportunities and experiences as those students from other neighboring districts. That led to the creation of a CentennialX: a human-centered design program where students work with real companies to create products, pitch those products, and present their work at conferences (like Stanford's MedX) around the country.

If we choose to let frustration and desperation get the better of us . . . then we choose to miss the silver lining:

Innovative ideas come out of frustration.

We tend to think of creativity and innovation as something that happens outside the box. But I would disagree. The most creative and innovative work comes from circumstances that force a new type of thinking for solutions inside the box.

It reminds me of the scene in *Apollo 13* when the carbon dioxide is building and they have to make a filter using only the materials inside the shuttle. There is pressure. There is frustration. And there is a group of desperate people working to create an innovative solution . . .

Put all the circumstances out on the table. Embrace the feelings of desperation and frustration. And then create something inside the box that is going to benefit everyone.

Because the only other option is to give in and give up. And that sure wouldn't be any fun!

Let's be honest. Being a teacher and school leader can be overwhelming.

There is so much to do (not enough time), so much to learn (where do we even start), and it all keeps changing.

But we want to make a difference. That's why we got into education. We want to be innovative, creative, and make a greater impact.

It's easy to say, but if you are like me, it is even easier to fall back into a pattern of what we've always done, instead of answering the question: **What is best for this learner in this situation?**

We are also surrounded by teachers, leaders, parents, and even students who are playing the game of school. It's been set up this way for years and it is hard to break decades of doing things "the way they always have been done" (even when we know it isn't best for kids).

That's why we often get a lot of resistance when we come up with **new ideas.** It's why there isn't always positive feedback when we try to **teach differently.** And, it's why **being innovative is not easy**, even if it is needed in our schools today.

This Book Is a Real Starting Point

I've written other education books, but *The PBL Playbook* is different. This book comes from another place of desperation and frustration. For years I've seen the transformative power of project-based learning experiences in my own classroom, in my colleagues' classrooms, and in countless learning places around the world.

Yet, for many teachers, including myself, it can be almost paralyzing to start the work of moving away from how we've always taught. I've made the mistake of sometimes writing up in the clouds (theory) instead of in the dirt (practical). While this can help us understand the WHY (which is important), it leaves us wanting to know HOW.

This book is about the HOW. You'll get step-by-step ideas and strategies to implement in your role as a teacher, coach, or leader tomorrow. You'll get ideas from over thirty different educators who were interviewed and shared their PBL tactics and best practices. You'll be able to apply this to your work, and most importantly to help transform the learning experiences our students have on a daily basis.

As a coach, I always believed that a playbook opened up the possibilities instead of limiting them. In *The PBL Playbook,* I hope to hit on that balance of providing enough guidance, support, and practical steps—while also allowing for the creativity and innovation inside each of you to shine through when designing, building, and running a project-based learning experience.

Are you ready to hit the ground running? Let's get started! You are one project away . . .

PART 1:
Not Just WHY, But HOW

CHAPTER 1:

Project-Based Learning Is a Start

XOXXOXOOXO

I was worried the first time I tried a project-based learning unit with my students. As a young teacher, I had prided myself on running a challenging class and had focused much of my attention on getting my students prepared for what we were both going to be assessed on: *the test.*

I was not doing test prep. I didn't believe that giving students sample test questions would make them do any better on our state-standardized scores (and still don't).

Yet I was actively trying to match my lessons and activities to what they would be assessed on later down the road. I thought that this was best practice and would benefit us both as they would be ready to tackle challenging questions (in any format) as we got toward the end of the school year.

Heading into our first true project-based learning unit, I wondered whether my students would learn as much as they did when I was teaching in more traditional methods.

I wondered if they would have more fun and balk at going back to those traditional tasks.

But, deep down, what I really worried about (if I'm being honest with myself) is how their results on the standardized test would reflect on me as a teacher.

And I don't think I was the only teacher who felt this way . . .

Is Practicing the Test the Best Way to Prepare for a Test?

As author Jay McTighe states: *"The logic of test prep is plausible and rooted in experience from other domains. For example, if you want to improve your performance in dribbling a basketball or piano playing, then you must practice those activities. Shouldn't the same apply to test taking?"*[3]

I was a former athlete and was a football and lacrosse coach during my time as a middle school and high school English/language arts teacher.

As a coach, I believed that winning was a by-product (not just a goal) of the time, work, and focus the team displayed while practicing. Fundamentals, teamwork, strategy, tactics, planning, and execution all had a role in how well the team performed. But at least we had common goals.

In the classroom, we had varying goals. Each student was different. They all had unique interests, ideas, friends, and views on what success looked like to them in school.

My goals as a teacher were fairly simple:

1. I wanted students to enjoy my class and find success in learning.
2. I wanted to challenge students and give them an opportunity to grow.
3. I wanted to make sure their hard work in my class showed on the learning assessments that were measured.

I say this because, maybe, just like me, you only have one or two assessments each year that are actually measured beyond your classroom walls.

And guess what?

We care about what we are measured on. We focus on it, and we try to improve it. This is not only teachers; this impacts every person in any field.

In a recent *Harvard Business Review* article, they talk about how the measures in other fields (CEOs, medicine, science, etc.) have the exact same impact:

> *It can't be that simple, you might argue—but psychologists and economists will tell you it is. Human beings adjust behavior based on the metrics they're held against. Anything you measure will impel a person to optimize his score on that metric. What you measure is what you'll get. Period.*
>
> *This phenomenon plays out time and again in research studies.*[4]

There is no way around it, except to change what we measure. Or, to change the game entirely.

I was caught up in a circle of practice that was based on some misconceptions on how to improve the metric I was judged on as a teacher. It is important to note that I was trying to do what was best for my students this entire time. I believe almost all teachers have the best interest of students, and that their practice is predicated on preparing students in any way possible.

McTighe shares the misconceptions that led me down this test prep trap as a young teacher, and what many of us commonly believe as the reasons for preparing students for a test that we don't believe in.

Misconception #1—The best (and only) way to improve test scores is to practice the test.

Here McTighe shares an analogy of the yearly physical exam with your doctor. Although the physician examines and measures your health, spending all your time trying to prepare for this physical with practice on the strategies would not make much sense.

> *It would be thought silly to practice the physical exam as a way to improve one's health. But this confusion is precisely what we see in schools all over North America. Local educators, fearful of results, focus on the indicators, not their causes. The format of the test misleads us, in other words.*[5]

Misconception #2—Standardized test items involve primarily recall and recognition, and thus drill and practice will be the most effective method to prepare students for them.

Grant Wiggins (2013) points out the flaw in this reasoning:

Even though the test format requires a selected response, it does not mean that the tested knowledge is necessarily simple. The [format] deceives you into thinking that since you are mimicking the format of the test, you are therefore mimicking the rigor of the test. But data show the opposite conclusively: local tests are often less rigorous than state and national tests even when they mimic the format.

Too often, the information revealed by test prep exercises identifies whether students have chosen the "correct" answer rather than helping teachers determine if they have a conceptual understanding of the underlying concepts and skills and can apply (transfer) those.[6]

How I Got Out of the Test Prep Trap with PBL

It started small.

First, I started to notice how disengaged my students were in class. Despite my efforts to use technology, create fun-learning activities, and challenge my students . . . I was failing them in many ways.

They cared more about getting a GRADE and playing the GAME of school than they did about learning. When I looked at the research, it was clear that it was not just my class (and my students) that were showing signs of apathy.

In a recent article by Scott McLeod on *Dangerously Irrelevant*, he shared results available from the annual Gallup poll of middle and high school students (over 9,20,000 students participated last fall). Here are a couple of key charts that Scott made from the data:[7]

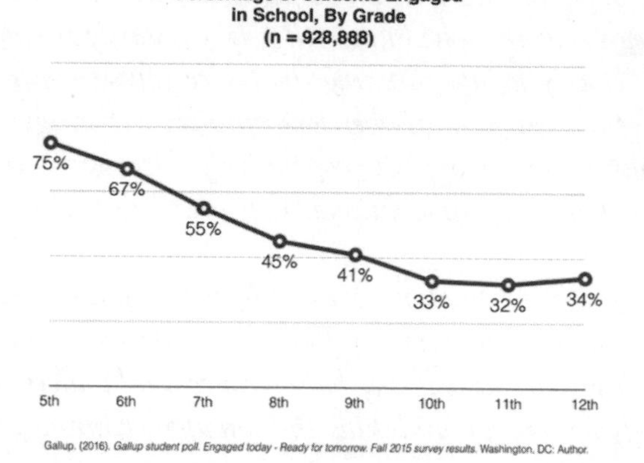

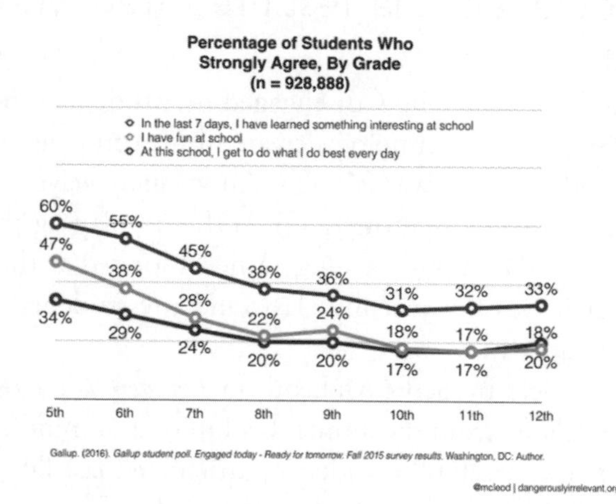

Interestingly enough, it seems that our students know this is happening. They know that they and their peers are often bored in school.

This was when I first started with project-based learning. It was a natural attempt at doing school differently, so my students might become engaged. At this point, I had nothing to lose.

My co-teacher and I taught our symbolism unit using an activity where students would create "junk sculptures" to represent characters, scenes, emotions, and much more through their creation. Our transfer goal was having them discuss in roundtables how the authors use the words on the page in the same way.

We got students talking during class, in real ways. Discussion games, fishbowl activities, and symposiums focused on their analysis out in the open, instead of trapped on the centered lines of a worksheet.

We changed our assessment of the human rights and genocide unit from being a letter to a state senator to developing, creating, and running an awareness campaign that would reach our community and people all across the country.

With each of the changes, my confidence grew as a teacher. With each new project, my students' confidence also grew in their ability to critically think, problem-solve, and create in authentic ways.

And they were not doing worse on standardized assessments. They did better.

They were not missing pieces of content that we could not cover because of lost time to the project. They were going deeper.

The Research Supports PBL Approach to Achievement

I wasn't the only one finding out how wrong I had been about Project-Based Learning. Everywhere I turned I started to see articles, journal reviews, and videos of teachers around the world who had seen their students achieve at high levels when moving from a traditional teaching approach to a PBL approach.

When Edutopia came out with this overview of the research around PBL, I nodded my head at the results:

> *Studies comparing learning outcomes for students taught via project-based learning versus traditional instruction show that when implemented well, PBL increases long-term retention of content, helps students perform as well as or better than traditional learners in high-stakes tests, improves problem-solving and collaboration skills, and improves students' attitudes towards learning.*[8] *PBL can also provide an effective model for whole-school reform.*[9]
>
> *A 2016 MDRC/Lucas Education Research literature review found that the design principles most commonly used in PBL align well with the goals of preparing students for deeper learning, higher-level thinking skills, and intra/interpersonal skills.*[10]

No longer could the argument be about how well (or poorly) students would do on standardized assessments. The research was clear. When PBL was implemented well, students thrived in traditional tests and in a wide variety of soft skills that are crucial to development and success beyond school.

The Buck Institute for Education also put out a research summary on PBL and twenty-first-century competencies that states,

> *Project Based Learning has been shown to yield a number of benefits for students, ranging from deeper learning of academic content to stronger motivation to learn. Looking specifically at how PBL supports 21st century learning goals, we can find several promising areas, including:*
>
> - *Academic Achievement*
> - *21st Century Competencies*
> - *Equity*
> - *Motivation*
> - *Teacher Satisfaction*[11]

I urge you to dive into this research more on the BIE website if you have any doubts.

If you asked any teacher, administrator, parent, school board member, student, or community member to list their top goals for an academic program, you would see achievement, twenty-first-century competencies, equity, and motivation all at the top.

Project-based learning is shown to work in all kinds of schools, in all different grade levels, with students of varying backgrounds and abilities.

So, if this is what the research says about PBL, then why do we still have so many schools falling into the test prep trap? Why do some many teachers feel like they cannot make the jump into PBL? Why haven't we seen a nationwide movement toward PBL as a best and effective practice for all students?

Finding the TIME for PBL When We Have to Cover So Much Material

When teachers ask me about my PBL experiences, they'll quickly ask three questions over and over again:

1. How did you find the time?
2. What about the curriculum?
3. How did you assess it and make sure students were understanding content, concepts, etc.?

In reality, this is just one question that I can phrase in a quick sentence:

How did you do PBL given the current constraints as a teacher in our educational system?

The issue is that we all have constraints. Are we supposed to as teachers and leaders NOT do Project-Based Learning because we don't have enough time . . . or can we start within the time we are given?

This isn't a case of all or nothing.

I think teacher and author Joy Kirr put it perfectly in this comment:

> *I cannot redesign my entire school like I know you dream of. I am one teacher. I can, however, with the blessings of my administration, give 60 minutes of my week over to the students. It is TOO LITTLE time, I know. And I can't make sure each project will change the world.* ***But it is a start.*** *And the lessons we all learn during this time seep into the other four hours I have with these students throughout the week, thank goodness. I don't have numbers to show student progress. But I'm trying to create lifelong learners. How do you measure that?*[12]

Project-based learning experiences give students opportunities that they would never have in school otherwise. To ME that is enough. It is enough to try this type of learning with your students. It is enough to take a risk and go beyond the curriculum.

I'd ask anyone who is criticizing PBL in the classroom to talk to the teachers and students who have had this opportunity. I'd ask them to look at what students are creating, making, and building during this time. I'd ask them to talk to the parents about their students' attitude toward learning.

I've heard from so many colleagues and teachers around the country (and world) who have said this time has changed their teaching and the way they view learning.

I give two answers to the question above:

1. Try it for a day and see what happens. Start small and build from there.
2. Teach through the project, instead of using the project as an "end-of-unit" assessment that takes more time than a multiple-choice test. When kids learn during the project, the time constraint goes away.

And yet, it also comes down to the school leaders. What do we praise, support, make time for, and allow as school leaders? Are we encouraging our staff and students to take risks and go beyond the traditional models of teaching and learning?

If you are a school leader, try to reflect on these four questions as a way to promote this type of learning in your school.

The First Question Is: What Do We Praise, Look For, and Assess?

There is a famous saying I referenced earlier: "What you measure is what matters." And this is very true in the teaching and learning world. If our schools are successful based only on standardized measures, then it is no coincidence that many focus their efforts on the performance of these measures. For our students, this tends to mean they believe handing work in on time, being compliant, and doing well on traditional assessments is what makes them a good student. It's why a third of my 11th graders during the 20% Project asked if they could just get a handout with a rubric instead of having to think for themselves on what they wanted to learn. Yet when we change what we praise and look for in a classroom, students begin to adjust what matters. When we praise failure, look for grit, and assess the process (instead of only the final product), then students are empowered to share their work and grow as learners in a variety of ways.

The Second Question Is: What Do We Support?

Take, for instance, a school that solely focuses on standardized assessments. The teachers are not supported by the administration by bringing in new ideas or curiosity to their profession. Then it is increasingly difficult for teachers to support students when they create or make. Often they'll never get the opportunity. Yet in schools like Wissahickon (where I taught) I was supported when I wanted to try something new in the classroom. Online and global opportunities like the Flat Classroom Project weren't looked down upon. And when my students wanted to try something outside of the box or run with a project idea, I jumped at supporting their innovative work through ideas like Project: Global Inform. Support is a key ingredient to help those *new ideas* actually *work.*

The Third Question Is: What Do We Make Time For?

A constant complaint I hear from teachers and students is that they don't have enough time. It drives stress levels up, and brings innovative work to a halt when we create curricula and schedules that are jam-packed with content and predetermined lessons. When we make time for reflection or self-assessment, sharing, and making/tinkering, our students (and our teachers) actually go out and TRY new things.

The Fourth Question Is: What Do We Allow?

What we allow for in our schools and classrooms will ultimately open up avenues for new ideas to develop. If we don't allow for inquiry, choice, collaboration, digital tools, failing, then usually only the people in charge are allowed to have ideas.

How to Teach about the Test and Learn beyond the Test

Around the testing time, when it came to be March, there started to be a real sense of urgency in my school. Are our kids ready to take this test? Have we done our best to prepare them for this assessment? And how can we figure out ahead of time what we need to do to get them there?

What always struck me as odd, is that we have all these tools and all this data that we can use, but we never have enough time. Instead of approaching the test as the ultimate measure of my ability to teach and my students' ability to learn, we began to take a different approach in my classroom and school.

Our focus was not to dismiss the test but to treat it as a reality.

The conversation I used to have with my students before the test was simple:

> *"I want you all to try your best on this, just like in anything else you do. But you should not be waking up in the middle of the night because of these tests. You should not be coming to school nervous because of these tests.*
>
> *You all, have been prepared for much greater things than these tests. The tests only show a smidgeon of your ability, not just as English students, but as human beings. So if you think that I'm going to stand up here and tell you how important these tests are, I'm not. Instead, you should treat them the same way you treat anything else. Do it to the best of your ability, and understand that everything you've been doing in my class has prepared you for this. But it has also prepared you for much more than this."*

My students scored well on our state tests. Not every single student, but across the board covering minority groups, low-economic groups, and all different types of students, they scored very well. In an effort to teach above the test, I had to look at my choices as a teacher with a different viewpoint.

Our focus needs to change. We can't hate these assessments. And we also can't love these assessments. We need to start treating these tests for what they really are, which is just one assessment out of many that our students will have to take in life.

Their first interview for a job, that's an assessment. The college essay they'll have to write, that's an assessment.

They are assessed every single day, and judged every single day, and this is just another assessment they'll have to take in the game of life.

Is Project-Based Learning the solution to all that is wrong with our current system? No.

But, it is a start. Like so many teachers around the world jumping into PBL, I saw my students get excited about learning again. I saw my students work together with their classmates toward common goals. I saw my students struggle and fight through tough learning moments. I saw my students become leaders and push their classmates to success. I saw them reflect on what worked, what didn't, and what they would do differently next time.

Above all, I saw my students LEARN. They demonstrated their understanding in all kinds of ways (and yes, the test was just one way). And, as a teacher, when we see our students learning, the excitement is contagious, and our creative spark continues well beyond the school day.

Go to THEPBLPLAYBOOK.com for more resources, materials, and guiding questions about this chapter.

CHAPTER 2:

How to Get Students Talking

XOXXOXOOXO

I remember the first time I heard the phrase "student-centered classroom," and I almost chuckled.

I had always believed my classroom was about the students; they were the reason we taught and my focus was always on their learning.

This new terminology sounded like another buzzword, and I didn't pay much attention to the presentation until I heard this:

Whoever is doing the talking is doing the majority of the learning. In your classroom what is the ratio of teacher-talk to student-talk?

I had never thought about this balance between teacher-talk to student-talk before. It made me reflect on how many of my lessons had me talking, entertaining, and presenting to my students. And, yet, as I continued to reflect, the best lessons were always the ones where students owned what they were learning and doing.

Whether it was a discussion, a project, or an activity—they were more engaged and empowered than when I was doing the entertaining.

I set off that year to give my students more of an opportunity to lead classroom discussions, have a choice in their projects, and ultimately make my classroom a student-centered space to learn and grow.

Then Reality Hit . . .

The idea of a student-centered classroom is great. Like most educational theories, it sounds doable, but then, in reality, it is challenging to get up and running.

One way to talk about changing to a student-centered classroom (and probably the most popular way to talk about this move) is to focus on getting rid of lectures. The lecture was a staple of classrooms for years and years but has always been a bit of a hot topic. Just recently the debate over lectures flared up again with Seth Godin taking issue with the stand-and-deliver mode of teaching on his blog:

> *In a recent NY Times op-ed, Susan Dynarski, a professor of education, public policy, and economics at the University of Michigan, describes why she has forbidden students from using laptops in her lectures.*
>
> *There's now plenty of data that shows that in a lecture setting, students with laptops don't do as well or learn as much as students without one. The reasons make sense, and I applaud her standards and her guts.*
>
> *But she missed the real issue.*[13]

How about this instead: No lecture hall.

Godin (an author of many best-selling books and founder of altMBA program) goes on to dispel many of the myths around lectures but ends on this piece that hit home:

A great teacher is smart enough and connected enough to run an interactive conversation, a participatory seminar in the concepts that need to be learned.

I agreed with this sentiment whole-heartedly. But when I first tried to move away from the usual lecture in my classroom, it was not easy.

In fact, I was awful at it.

I struggled to get the students involved. I didn't have an answer for when the room went silent (when they were supposed to be leading a discussion), and the project-based learning that had all the choices became a madhouse of options that were too hard to assess and too broad to connect to what we were learning.

Later that year, in a conversation with a great mentor teacher of mine (love you, Jen Smith!), she asked me a very simple question:

How did you scaffold the change? Or did you just jump into students owning their learning headfirst?

I attempted to respond with the ways I scaffolded this change until I realized I had nothing to say.

Crickets

After admitting my faults as someone who tends to jump in headfirst, she laughed and said, "Let's start with where the kids are at and what they are used to. Then, where we want them to be. All we have to do after that is plan steps to move them from point A to B."

The Three-Step System for Getting Students to Do the Talking

Most of my students were used to a teacher lecturing and then asking a few questions during the lecture. They would either raise a hand to answer or sometimes "turn and talk" to discuss in a small group.

For project-based learning, most of my students were used to a very detailed project outline, with step-by-step directions that were more like a recipe than a wide-open project. They would get a rubric that was geared toward the final product, and rarely had anything to do with the process of learning.

I was throwing these kids into projects like our "Junk Sculpture Project" where they had to create a sculpture (using household items and junk) that represented various symbols and motifs in a recent short story. The rubric was process driven, and there was not a 14-step process for the kids to follow; it was a project they could modify to their needs, but instead, the kids were lost and not sure how to proceed.

Similarly, I was putting these kids into a Socratic seminar where I did none of the talking and they discussed with their own questions, insights, ideas, and answers as a large group.

Most of the time during this Socratic seminar it was dead-silent or dominated by a few students who ran the conversation.

In order to get my students to take ownership in their learning, we started where they were at, instead of where I wanted them to be.

We began by focusing on the classroom discussion habits. Most kids were answering only questions that I asked with an answer to that question.

They weren't asking their own questions of why, how, when, where, and who. They weren't sharing what they "think," what they "know," and what they "connected to" during the discussion.

In reality, they were just focused on getting the right answer. And we set out to fix this during the first step to a student-centered classroom.

Step #1: The Discussion Game

My students rolled into class like any other day, and not much was changed. The tables were still set up in small groups, and the projector was on with their "Do Now" activity on the board. And the homework for the week was written for each day.

The only difference was that each seat had a white envelope on it, filled with five cards of all different colors.

This was the opening of our first discussion game. I got the idea from our colleague Melisa Perlman and have seen variations of this game all over the place online. The best part about it is that it is simple to create, simple to explain, and completely modifiable depending on your subject, grade level, or classroom setting.

Here're the basics. Each student gets a number of different-colored cards to use throughout the discussion. They must play each card once but can play the question card multiple times after using all other cards.

Red Card = I think

Blue Card = I know (because)

Yellow Card = Pose a Question

Green Card = I feel

Orange Card = Connect (to yourself, to the world, to another text/idea/subject)

Each card is worth a point (if you want to grade this activity, completely up to you and your classroom/school), and the goal is to replace assessing only the final product (quiz) and instead the process of learning (having an active discussion).

This scaffolds the student-centered classroom in two ways.

First, the game is centered on your subject, concept, content, and text for the lesson. Students have to be engaged with that content in order to respond with the above answers and questions (I think, I know because, I feel, connect, etc.).

Second, it models the many ways you can contribute to an active learning discussion. This helps the students who may be shy or want to hide during the discussion.

Finally, we added a back-channel component to this game where students did not have to always talk out loud to the class to discuss and earn points, but could "play their cards" online in platforms like Todays Meet.com for participating in the discussion.

Step #2: The Fish Bowl

After playing the discussion game a few times, students began to get into discussions and own the conversation. Yes, they were prodded into answers and asking questions, but the goal of the first step is to get them talking (and have me talk way less).

It worked for our class and for many in our school. But, it was not the final goal. I'd rather not have the carrot (or stick) be the only reason students are talking, so we had to continue moving away from that reason, and also change up the format to one that is less scripted by the cards.

Enter the Fish Bowl.

This activity was used by our colleague Anthony Gabriele, and like all good things, we modified it to work with our group of students. There are some good write-ups online for the Fish Bowl (like this one) and many different ways to do it, but here is how we did it in my class as the second step.

Fish Bowl Prep: Students are to have read, learned, or already delved into a specific text or content before the start of class. This, however, does not need to be homework. It could be learning that happened in a previous lesson or experience. The key is that the students are not learning something "new" during the Fish Bowl; they are instead going to learn from each other during the discussion and share their insights and questions (much like the discussion game).

Classroom Setup: Set up your classroom with two sets of circles. One big circle will be on the outside, and then on the inside there will be a smaller circle of four-to-five chairs (depending on class size, this could also be three or six chairs).

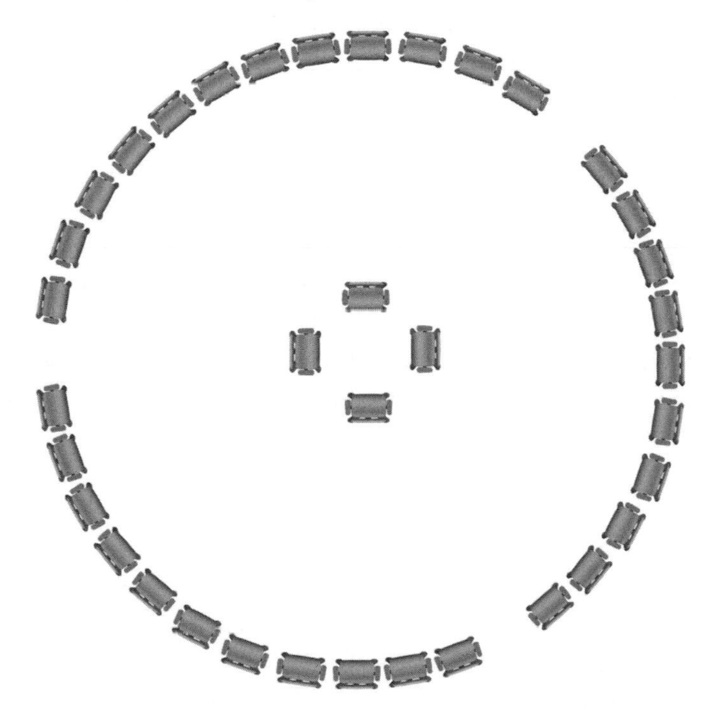

How it works: When students come into class, they will grab a seat. Don't worry where they sit, as all students will eventually get into the middle of the circle (The Fish Bowl) for the discussion. The **inside circle** does the talking and discussing. They should be prepared but focus on having an active conversation using the techniques learned in the discussion game. The **outside circle** takes notes on the inner discussion. This could be scaffolded by the teacher to focus on specific areas of the conversation, or more wide open like taking notes during a lecture. Depends on your situation for how you want to prep students for the outside not taking.

Every five minutes you'll want to replace the inner circle with new students to discuss. They can pick up where the previous discussion left off, or start new.

Two keys to making this work. First, as a teacher, you must not prompt or get students talking. The goal is for them to have a productive struggle in the beginning and then get into a flow. Second, depending on your class, you may want to pick the fishbowl groups ahead of time to get a good mix of students for the discussion. This, of course, is your preference as the teacher.

Finally, you can assess this conversation in a few ways, but I'd focus more on the active discussion part than what was said at first. Then as you do it more often and students become comfortable, you can change a rubric to have different assessment pieces that reflect the content of the discussion.

**Note:* As with the Discussion Game, you can add an online component to this as well. Have the outside of the circle write their feedback and notes on a shared doc, a backchannel like TodaysMeet, and discussion board forum inside an LMS, or any other way to make the note-taking more collaborative.

Step #3: The Symposium

When students have successfully played the discussion game and then moved onto the Fish Bowl, you've already got them to do most of the talking. This is a win (and should be celebrated)!

But remember our original goal?

Student-centered, where they are asking and answering the questions, learning from each other, and having a choice in where they head with their learning.

The Symposium is the final step in the scaffolding to get kids to do the talking.

At first glance, the Symposium looks much like the Fish Bowl. The classroom is set up the same with two circles (one smaller inside). But, this time the prep is different.

Students will get into groups of three to six to prepare for their symposium discussion. The discussion will be twenty minutes long where they will share their insights, connections, commentary, and questions on the content. As a group, they can prep together or separately for this discussion.

The outside circle plays an important role in the symposium. They take notes the first 20 minutes, but then they get to "grill" the inner circle with questions for the next 15–20 minutes. This takes the inner conversation to the next level with a back and forth between the entire class.

As a teacher, you sometimes have to play moderator during this second part of the symposium.

The fun is seeing the students do the talking, the question asking, the debating, and the learning. This is what I was hoping to see when I first did a Socratic Seminar, but it did not work, mainly due to the fact that I did not scaffold a way for students to slowly get into the habit of doing the talking.

It doesn't matter if you look at Bloom's Taxonomy, Webb's Depth of Knowledge, or any other set of educational standards or guidelines.

When students are communicating and collaborating (and talking), much more learning is happening!

This is the three-step system we used and it worked well but constantly needed to be tweaked.

It looked very different in terms of setup and time allotted when I did it with different groups of students depending on their age, level, and experience in a student-centered environment.

As we begin to explore PBL opportunities in our curriculum and classes as a teacher, we have to start with the basics of collaboration, communication, critical thinking, and creativity. To that end, having students work together in meaningful ways is a step we do not want to jump over or miss along the way.

Go to THEPBLPLAYBOOK.com for more resources, materials, and guiding questions about this chapter.

CHAPTER 3:

Dipping Our Toes into PBL with an Activity That Works

XOXXOXOOXO

In our last chapter, we dove into a three-step system to get students to do the talking. Getting them to open up and do the majority of talking (and learning) is not as easy as some make it out to be.

In fact, for me, it was incredibly difficult.

The three-step system scaffolded a way for students to take on more and more of the discussion responsibilities until they were ready to take over. Here are the three steps in a nutshell:

THREE-STEP SYSTEM TO GET KIDS TO DO THE TALKING

Now that I had students talking in my classes, I also wanted to get them creating, making, and designing.

But, I had the same problem with project-based learning that I did with getting students to own the discussion and do the talking (instead of me doing all the talking).

I was really bad at scaffolding PBL opportunities for my students to own that process as well. Too often my scaffolding was me "telling them" what to do.

Most of the "project-based learning" I had my students do, looked something like this:

1. Teach the students about a concept or particular content.
2. Have them demonstrate their learning in various ways.
3. Give them an end-of-the-unit project.
4. Provide detailed steps to complete the project in a handout.
5. Provide detailed unit to assess the project in a handout.
6. Give students a detailed time line on when things should be done for the project.
7. Help students navigate project.
8. Collect student projects.
9. Notice that all their projects look eerily similar, almost like they were following a recipe.
10. Grade the projects and hand them back with feedback.
11. Repeat.

The problem with these projects was the recipelike nature that happened when students began handing things in.

My students were still just trying to follow the rules, instead of actually creating something on their own that they could be proud about.

During one of these projects (when students had inevitably gone through the motions) I had to ask my students the question:

What was the last project or school assignment you did that left you with a feeling of accomplishment?

The responses all fell into two categories:

1. Students were accomplished when they received a grade higher than what they expected to receive and/or if the class was known as difficult and challenging.

2. Projects where they had choice in what they were creating and solving (there weren't that many with this response). Most of them said this happened outside of school.

I wondered how I could do project-based learning in my class where students would be challenged, engaged, and also inspired to do great work they would be proud of (instead of only work that would get them a grade) . . .

How My View on Project-Based Learning Changed

You ever have one of those moments where you wonder what you are doing with your life? I mean, at the very least, you are like me and have had times where something catches you off guard and makes you rethink your purpose and impact on the world.

This happened when Patrick Larkin shared a video of students in his school district who created a PSA (Public Service Announcement) that went viral online. In the video (shared here: http://ajjuliani.com/lets-change-the-world-with-our-students-heres-how/) the students use paper and their phone to record a silent PSA to end the use of the "R-word" in our schools and in our daily lives. It really spoke to me seeing how much of an impact these students could have on their world while still in school (seventh grade).

The project itself was so simple.

First, choose a problem in your school that is also impacting the world.

Then, figure out how to solve this problem and share your solution with your classmates, school, and the world.

They didn't need to use fancy technology. They used only printed out paper with text (could have written it by hand) and a phone to video their PSA.

The key was the final piece. Share their PSA project with the world. This authentic audience kept the students engaged and empowered them to create something that mattered more than fridge art.

I realized that this type of short project is exactly how you can scaffold PBL for students of any age.

How to Scaffold PBL So Students Are Ready

PBL FOR EVERY CLASSROOM

Before jumping into Design Challenges, Maker Projects, and Genius Hour, I would always do an activity that followed the simple process shared above. This PSA project can be done in any subject and in any grade level (with modifications, of course).

I'll break down the example PSA Project that I use all of the time in workshops to show how this is possible. The key elements are that you choose content that you want the students to learn, but give them a choice in which content they choose.

After that, the project is simple.

Research what the world needs to know about ____, and what they can do about _____.

Then create a PSA to demonstrate that information and understanding.

For my example, I want my students to learn about the United Nations 2030 Goals. So it would look like this:

Research what the world needs to know about one of the UN 2030 GOALS, and what they can do about _____.

Here is the step-by-step process for scaffolding PBL with a PSA Project:

Step #1: Present the Content that Students Are Going to Learn (Then Give Choice on Which Area They Learn More About)

Note: Some students will have background knowledge; others may not have much background knowledge, and that is okay.

For this example, I give learners the topic of the UN 2030 Goals. The content they are going to learn is about these UN 2030 Goals (which works well because most folks don't have a deep understanding or much knowledge about the goals).

Second, I ask them to get into small groups (two to three people) and choose a goal that resonates with them personally. This is key because the more meaningful and relevant the activity becomes, the more effort and commitment the team will have toward the project.

It's also important to note that I do not give a lot of time for this activity. Thirty minutes max amount of time. It should be a one-class activity in school where time and resources may be limited.

Step #2: Have Students Research the Content (What Does the World Need to Know about It and What Can They Do about It)

Once the goal (content) has been chosen, it's time to research! The key here is to research quickly and efficiently.

If you have younger kids, provide stations that have bits and pieces of the research ready to consume. Things like videos, articles, pictures, graphs are key to giving young students a headstart on the research.

If you have older students (or adult learners), feel free to point them toward a couple of websites or directions to research online. For the UN 2030 Goals, I always choose GlobalGoals.org as a starting place.

3. Learn Fast, Research Quickly

Research about your chosen UN 2030 Goal & start Writing down what the World needs to know.

The other important piece to remember during this research step is that you must give a specific time of how long (or else they'll get stuck in more and more research). You have to also give very specific things they are looking for (such as what the world needs to know about the 2030 goal and what they can do about it to help out).

Step #3: Create a PSA

Here is where we climb up the Bloom's Taxonomy and get students making and creating. When you use this activity with a specific piece of content (2030 Goals, Periodic Table of Elements, historical figures, scenes from a play, author study, etc.), the project becomes about demonstrating your understanding of this content through creating the PSA.

4. Create Something That Matters
(a PSA about 30--90 seconds long)

a. Write Script
b. Put it on paper
c. Film it with your phone!
(or use other tech to create)

You can give the option of creating a PSA much like the one shared above (The R-Word) or learners can create it with video, with a slideshow, a skit, or any other type of way to spread their knowledge and understanding.

We are scaffolding PBL here so a key point to remember during the creation stage is that many times students will want to mimic or copy what they saw as the example (or exemplar) given to the whole class.

This is something to keep an eye on, but also a teaching moment. I always share Austin Kleon's good versus bad copying chart[14] to get my students thinking about personalizing their PSAs and projects:

Once students are finished creating, the project is not yet done! Two key pieces remain. First, they have to share this with a bigger audience than just themselves and their classmates.

Sharing it with the world gives the students an authentic audience. As a teacher, I'd try to find various audiences for my students to share their work with, but sometimes throwing it up on YouTube and social media is enough to get the positive peer pressure working!

5. Share It With The World!

-Tweet out the video
-Put it on Facebook
-Put it on YouTube

Finally, you'll want to have the students reflect on what they learned, what they created, and what they would do differently.

This reflection continues the learning well after the "project" has been completed.

The final product should never be the end of a learning experience, only the beginning of the next learning experience.

Don't Just Teach What You Know, Teach What You Are Learning

When starting students on a journey with Project-Based Learning, we can think of it as a journey where the travel is just as important as the destination.

Learning happens during the project work and as a result of the work, just as taking a hike up a mountain is as important as getting to the final destination of that view over the valley.

The mark of many great projects is that the learners teach what they know and understand through the project.

But, you don't need to be an expert in order to teach.

The goal here is for students to be documenting, sharing, creating, and teaching while they are learning.

This process enables a constant reflection and dialogue to take place between the learning, the collaborator, the mentor, the teacher, and the audience.

That is what makes true PBL so authentic. It is the connections we can make throughout the learning process that do not happen when sitting in a seat listening to a lecture, or sitting in a seat answering multiple-choice questions.

Go to THEPBLPLAYBOOK.com for more resources, materials, and guiding questions about this chapter.

CHAPTER 4:

Simple System for Planning PBL Experiences

XOXXOXOOXO

The most successful teaching begins, therefore, with clarity about desired learning outcomes and about the evidence that will show that learning has occurred.

—Grant Wiggins and Jay McTighe, *The Understanding by Design Guide to Creating High-Quality Units*

There is something happening across the country and around the world right now. It's hidden in the planning sessions of colleagues, in the professional development opportunities at schools and conferences, and in the hallways as teachers and administrators talk with each other about their students.

It's been happening in pockets for so long that now those groups of teachers and leaders are starting to bring in new teachers and new leaders to build a true culture of learning that looks and feels different.

It's taking shape as a revolution of sorts (but not some type of education reform) that is beginning to make its way into every school and every classroom.

The textbooks are no longer "good enough," and the multiple-choice tests are no longer "good enough," and the lectures are no longer "good enough" for our kids.

We've seen what can happen when students are presented with a problem to solve, a challenge to overcome, and a learning experience that is both relevant and meaningful to them as an individual and citizen.

We've seen what can happen when students own their learning, have a choice in the process and performance task, and get to choose how they can demonstrate understanding.

Project-based learning (PBL) is no longer relegated to gifted classrooms, honors classes, and exploratory specials. PBL is an active piece of the K-12 learning experience, found in every subject, in every grade level, and in every part of curricula and scope and sequences.

PBL is taking over traditional finals and midterms as the performance task. It is showing up as HOW you teach the unit, instead of only an ending project to the unit. PBL is growing because it engages and empowers students to learn experientially and share that learning in new and unique ways that go well beyond the classroom.

Yet, many teachers are asking: How do we plan and implement PBL? How do we "fit it in" our current curriculum? How do we assess it using our current grading guidelines? How do we manage this type of learning?

These are all real concerns and questions that cannot be dismissed. PBL takes time to plan, implement, manage, and assess. Then it takes time to tweak, improve, and highlight.

In this chapter we are going to focus on the planning process of PBL, and how to jump into it quickly when inspiration strikes!

Note: There are many fantastic resources out there for PBL Planning, including the Buck Institute for Education's website and resources, and *Hacking Project Based Learning*'s Ross Cooper and Erin Murphy's site with resources and planning templates. I urge you to check them out and see how they might be of guidance during your PBL journey!

This planning process I am going to share takes five steps to start PBL with your students. It does not go into the management or assessment (as we will talk a bit more about that in upcoming chapters). Here's the simple system to plan out your PBL:

1. Start with a Problem/Challenge/Inquiry

Here's where we begin: **A reason for project-based learning.**

Many folks will tell you to start with the curriculum, or with the standards, or with an enduring question/understanding; however, the best PBL experiences I've been a part of did not start there, but instead started with a reason.

When my students helped design Project: Global Inform, it was out of a need to actually DO something about current human rights violations. When Vicki Davis and Julie Lindsay created the Flat Classroom Project, it was out of a need to have global collaboration while students were in school. When teachers at my district created CentennialX, it was out of a need to give students authentic opportunities to solve problems.

Great PBL experience comes from a place of need and interest. What problem can students solve? What challenge can be presented as an opportunity to create something of value? What curiosities and inquiry do students already have that can lead to a PBL experience?

As BIE outlines in their definition of PBL:

> ***Project-Based Learning*** *is a teaching method in which students gain knowledge and skills by working for an extended period of time to investigate and respond to an authentic, engaging, and complex question, problem, or challenge.*[15]

Let's work backward by thinking about the reasons (and the WHY for PBL) that connect to a problem, challenge, or inquiry. This ultimately allows you as a teacher to start from a place of meaning and relevancy before going into any other areas of planning.

2. What Are Students Going to Learn? What Skills Will They Acquire and Master?

The second step of this system is to identify what the students are going to learn during this PBL experience. This is when you look at the curriculum, standards, and skills that align with the content area information that is going to be a part of this process.

While it may seem a bit difficult at first, I want to provide an example.

Let's say you are teaching fourth grade. Your students are excited to tackle the challenge of getting kids in the cafeteria to actually recycle with regularity! That is a great challenge and problem to tackle, but how does it connect to your standards and curriculum?

Here is where you can unpack the standards and current curriculum that you have. The research to find best practices for recycling connects too many standards. The reading, writing, and viewing also connect to standards. The designing, prototyping, and creating of a new recycling can or system connects to standards.

Maybe you can link this PBL experience to a social studies unit that talks about the rise of recycling. Maybe it links to a nonfiction part of your language arts curriculum. Maybe the scientific process can be used to connect to your science or STEM curriculum. And of course, the planning and creation can be linked to a piece of the math curriculum.

Every school and district is different, but if we are going to make the switch to PBL, we must not forget that our focus is on what skills and knowledge students can acquire and master in order to help prepare for their future.

3. What Will Students Make, Create, and Design? Who Are They Creating for and Why?

Now that we've got the major problem students will be solving, and the connection to curriculum and standards, the focus of our planning moves to what students will be making and who they will be making it for (as part of their authentic audience).

For this, I turn to authors Ross Cooper and Erin Murphy, and how they describe the variety of option for PBL in their book, *Hacking Project Based Learning*:

> *PBL can unfold in a variety of ways. Teachers should choose a track based on the needs of their students, their readiness as facilitators, and the demands of the curriculum. While it would be unrealistic to detail every possible track, below are the three we find are most common:*

- ***Product Track (most restrictive)***—*In a project completed with fourth-grade students, each group was expected to produce a pinball machine. The difference between this experience and a traditional project is that the journey to the product looked different depending on each group's creative decisions and trials and errors. Students learned about electricity & magnetism and force & motion through their work.*
- ***Problem Track (medium restrictive)***—*In this scenario, the project is initiated by presenting students with a problem, or in some cases, the students may identify the problem themselves. Examples may include how to tackle the dilemma of subpar cafeteria food, or students being asked to identify a problem of importance to their age group. Student work would then revolve around identifying the cause of the issue and proposing or enacting a remedy.*
- ***Open-Ended Track (least restrictive)***—*Here the project begins with the teacher sharing the High Impact Takeaways/ enduring understandings and possibly the Umbrella/essential question with the class. Students then design a project that is truly medium agnostic. In other words, they can demonstrate their knowledge however they choose. For example, a high school physics teacher may share the High Impact Takeaway/ enduring understanding: An electric current can produce a magnetic field and a changing magnetic field can produce an electric current. Students, with teacher guidance, then design a project that will support this understanding. Simply researching and sharing information would not be sufficient.*[16]

In each track, the students own the problem and can solve it in many different ways. Yet, depending on the class, the age, the subject, and the time constraints, a teacher can set up and plan for a PBL experience that will align with the reality of their situation.

4. How Can You Scaffold and Structure the Experience?

In *Setting the Standard for Project Based Learning* (ASCD 2015), authors John Larmer, John Mergendoller, and Suzie Boss present a framework for the Gold Standard PBL that includes Essential Project Design Elements and Project Based Teaching Practices.

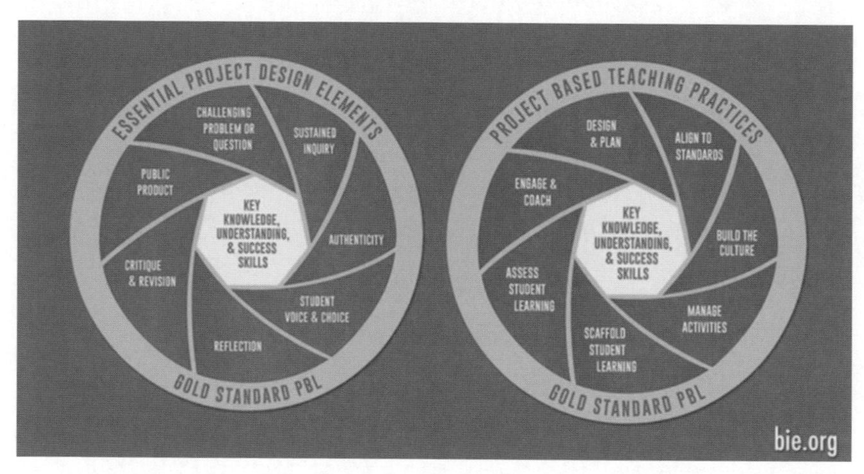

In planning for PBL, the teacher must take an active role in not only looking at these elements but also acknowledging that it is going to be challenging work for the students that needs to be structured and scaffolded along the way.

We've already planned for what they are going to solve, how it connects to standards and skills, and what they will be making. But, a major piece in the planning process is putting together a structure that gives students voice and choice, while also holds them accountable with checks for understanding, benchmarks, and opportunities to iterate.

I'm a bit biased toward using the Design Thinking process to structure and scaffold PBL (check out TheLaunchCycle.com for more on this), but Design Thinking is one of many ways we can structure a PBL experience.

You may use the engineering process, the scientific method, the inquiry cycle, or a process that works specifically within your content and with your students.

The key here is to have this planned out before students get started, and present them with a timeline of the project. You may be flexible throughout the project, but these guidelines will help students plan out their work, and give you spots to check for understanding along the way.

5. When Will Students Self-Assess, Revise, and Reflect?

During Project-Based Learning, we can all fall into the trap of trying to race to the finish line at the last moment. The first few PBL experiences with my students went something like this:

> *I gave my students free reign over when they did their work, with only a final deadline for the completion of the project. Only to find out that most of them procrastinated till the last night, and finished the day before the project was due.*

How could I blame them?! You could find me doing the same thing when I was in school and especially when I was getting my master's degree in grad school. Procrastination is an easy trap to fall into, and it is also a powerful motivator.

Above we talked about a structure for PBL. But I would go a step further in your planning and build in specific times for students to self-assess, to reflect on their work, and to revise. Don't wait till the end of the project to do these extremely important learning tasks.

While we aren't going to dive into assessment in this chapter, I'd also say that a big piece of planning out PBL is realizing that we are going to have to assess not just the final product, but also the process, and most importantly the learning.

Planning for these times before the project begins will only help you as the teacher (and help the students) when it comes time to assess their work.

Go to THEPBLPLAYBOOK.com for more resources, materials, and guiding questions about this chapter.

CHAPTER 5:

Running and Managing the PBL Classroom

XOXXOXOOXO

You've read the blog posts, tweets, and articles (and even some books).

Maybe you've even attended some conferences or seen someone speak live.

They say, "Project-based learning changed my role as a teacher. I could talk to more students. I became a guide and coach instead of talking at kids all day."

And you think, that sounds awesome! It sounds like a dream classroom.

So, you start.

You find a PBL lesson or unit to do with your class.

The kids are excited. Or maybe they are nervous. Or maybe they just want a worksheet. In any case, you and the students jump into this new experience ready for anything.

As the project continues, you begin to feel more and more overwhelmed.

How can I talk to every kid and every group? How can I manage all these different projects happening at the same time? How can I grade and assess the work the students are doing while still being supportive and challenging them to take risks?

Then it hits. Pure panic.

You wonder why you started down this path in the first place. The class feels out of control. The projects aren't going as planned, and you are in too deep to stop now!

If you are feeling this way or have ever felt this way, then you've joined all of us that have made the switch to PBL in our classrooms.

It can be tough! In fact, it is downright scary sometimes to give up control, allow for students to go off the beaten path, and really work through a problem to solve.

But I'm here to say that it can be done. That even though you may give up some creative control, you'll still have to make sure there is structure during the project and help provide that for students. Here are four ways to help manage the PBL experience and make it one that allows for your role to morph into the Guide on the Ride, instead of Guide on the Side.

Four Ways to Manage Project-Based Learning

1. You Can Give Choice and Ownership While Still Providing a Clear Structure

One of the first things I learned about PBL was that the traps were on opposite sides of the spectrum.

Trap #1 was giving eighteen specific steps for students to follow with an extremely detailed rubric. While the project would be very structured, you would also get back the exact same project product from every student (or group). Chris Lehmann calls this "recipe-based learning," not project-based learning.

We want students to be chefs, not cooks.

However, Trap #2 is giving too much freedom in structure, time, and checkpoints. This leads to stalling at certain points and never getting to the actual creation piece (or getting there too quickly).

I've tinkered with all different types of ways to structure PBL but have fallen in love with Design Thinking as a framework for the creative process.

The LAUNCH Cycle outlines creative work from start to finish. From listening and learning to navigating ideas, to highlight what works, the LAUNCH Cycle builds capacity and clarity for teachers and students who are making, building, tinkering, and creating.

Here are the phases as we describe them in our book, *LAUNCH*:

L: Look, Listen, and Learn

In the first phase, students look, listen, and learn. The goal here is awareness. It might be a sense of wonder at a process or an awareness of a problem or a sense of empathy toward an audience.

A: Ask Tons of Questions

Sparked by curiosity, students move to the second phase, where they ask tons of questions. They can share these questions with friends, teachers, mentors, and the world (especially online sites like Quora).

U: Understanding the Process and/or Problem

This leads to understanding the process or problem through an authentic research experience. They might conduct interviews or needs assessments, research articles, watch videos, or analyze data. During this phase, they are constantly putting their work out for others to look at and give feedback.

N: Navigate Ideas

Students apply that newly acquired knowledge to potential solutions. In this phase, they navigate ideas. Here they not only brainstorm but also analyze ideas, combine ideas, and generate a concept for what they will create.

C: Create a Prototype

In this next phase, they create a prototype. It might be a digital work or a tangible product, a work of art or something they engineer. It might even be an action or an event or a system.

H: Highlight and Fix

Next, they begin to highlight what's working and fix what's failing. The goal here is to view this revision process as an experiment full of iterations, where every mistake takes them closer to success. As they share what they've made, the feedback they receive will be key to the revision process.

Launch to an Audience

Then, when it's done, it's ready to launch. In the launch phase, they send it to an authentic audience. They share their work with the world!

This was the piece of the 20% Project and future projects I did with my students (like Project: Global Inform, 2030 Schools, Flat Classroom Project, NetGenEd Project)—that took it to the next level!

2. Every Student/Group Needs an Action Plan

Yes, that's right. It doesn't matter if you are working with five-year-olds or eighteen-year-olds. PBL requires an action plan. What is going to be learned, created, and shared? When is it going to be completed by? Who is going to be responsible? What barriers and obstacles might be in the way? What resources are needed?

Now this is going to look different at each level, but the goal is to have students outline what they are going to accomplish (and when) before they actually start.

It's backward design for students, and it helps them create goals and a structure for their creative work.

Action Plan Template

Action step: What will be done?	**Responsibilities:** Who?	**Timeline:** When will it be done? day/month	**Resources:** What do we have? What do we need?	**Potential issues:** What are the concerns? Proactive steps?
Step 1: Planning				
Step 2:				
Step 3:				
Step 4:				
Step 5:				
Step 6:				
Step 7:				
Step 8:				
Step 9:				

The best benefit of an action plan is that it gives the teachers and the students common places to have checkpoint conversations and conferences throughout the project.

Which leads to our next way to manage PBL.

3. Short Conferences That Pack a Punch

Conferences are one of the most underutilized approaches to managing a PBL experience. However, they can be extremely practical and powerful when done with a purpose.

And (key point here), they don't need to be a long and arduous process for teacher or student.

I love how author and professor John Spencer lays out the three types of student conferences:

THREE TYPES OF STUDENT CONFERENCES

	FEEDBACK	REFLECTION	MASTERY
THE FOCUS	TARGETED HELP	STUDENT SELF-REFLECTION	MASTERY TOWARD STANDARDS
TEACHER ROLE	ANSWER QUESTIONS	ASK QUESTIONS	ASK AND ANSWER
STUDENT ROLE	ASK QUESTIONS	ANSWER QUESTIONS	ASK AND ANSWER

The Feedback conference happens during the process as the student or group is asking for help and insight from the teacher.

The Reflection conference happens after they have completed one of the steps in the action plan as the teacher asks questions to check for understanding.

The Mastery conference happens throughout the process as both the students and the teacher understand what is being assessed and what is the goal.

4. Having Students Reflect and Document on a Weekly Basis

Project management should not fall entirely on the shoulders of a teacher. When students are working their way through a problem to solve, there will be many times they have to reroute, shift perspectives, try something new, or throw out an approach that wasn't working.

If they have to ask permission every time they do this, then a teacher will be bogged down in answering the specific requests.

If they do not ask permission and don't share the changes, the teacher will often be left behind on where the project is headed and how they can help guide.

This is where sharing, document, and reflecting come into play as a specific way to help manage PBL.

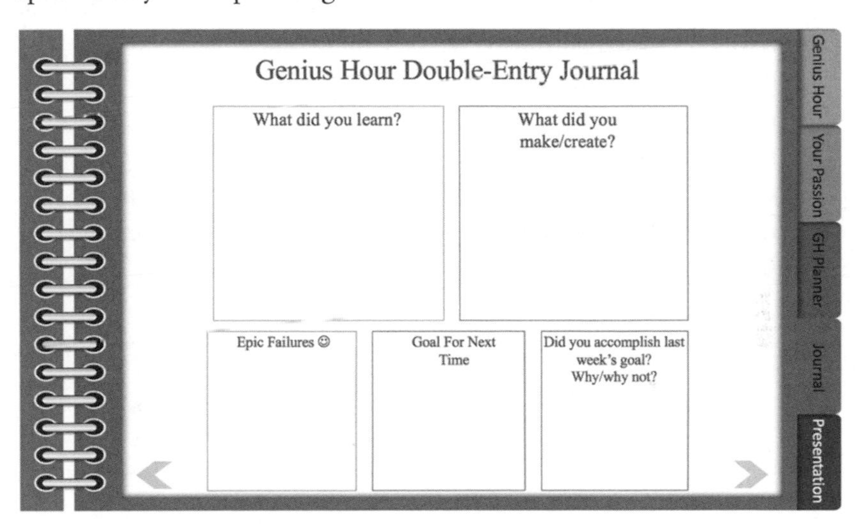

As the above picture shows, one of the ways my students reflected during Genius Hour was to answer questions about what they learned, what they made, what goals they had, and what went well (as well as what things they tried that did not work out).

We've had students reflect and document their project using all kinds of tools and forms. Blogs, podcasts, vlogging using tools such as SoundCloud, WordPress, Seesaw, YouTube, and Flipgrid.

The key is to have students reflect, share, and document in a place that you have access to as a teacher.

Sometimes it can be as simple as a Google Form or shared Google Doc.

Here you can follow along with the project, giving comments as needed, and checking in with students or groups who may need some extra attention that class period or week.

Bringing It All Together

Ultimately, we want PBL to feel as real and authentic as possible.

That does not mean that we get rid of deadlines. We have them in the real world!

It does not mean that we get rid of checkpoints and benchmarks. We have them in the real world!

It does not mean we get rid of formative and informal conversations. You get the point.

Our goal is not only to guide students on their learning journey but also to be a resource on things that go well beyond content and skills (such as time management, how to reach out to mentors, getting through a rough patch, and communication).

Go to THEPBLPLAYBOOK.com for more resources, materials, and guiding questions about this chapter.

CHAPTER 6:

Authentic Research during Project-Based Learning

XOXXOXOOXO

Both of my sons love playing soccer. I grew up watching football and played soccer only very briefly (at the youth level) before going all in on American football throughout middle school and high school.

I watch football all of the time, coached football for years, and taught both of my boys how to throw a football (properly) by the time they turned three.

We, by all accounts, are a football household who watches every Philadelphia Eagles game (Super Bowl Champs!) and a lot of college football as well.

But here we are with both of my sons playing soccer, loving the sport, and wanting to watch it.

And I was at a loss.

It's not that I don't appreciate the game of soccer. I do. I love watching the World Cup, and I've played my fair share of FIFA video game over the years, but that wasn't the problem.

The problem is that I didn't KNOW anything about soccer.

I didn't know the difference between the Premier League, La Liga, and the Champions League. I didn't know who were good teams, or good players, beyond the Messis and Ronaldos of the world.

I wanted to know more about soccer and I started Googling around and guess what happened?

Information overload.

Too much at once and I couldn't really follow it.

So, I jumped onto Instagram and followed two soccer accounts (BrFootball and PremiereLeague).

Within two days I understood the difference between leagues. Another five days and I had a grasp on who the best players were. A couple of more days and I understood who were all the top teams in each of Europe's major leagues. Who had qualified for the Champions League and who the past winners were (and who was expected to win).

I "researched" all about soccer and performed only ONE web search that got me little to no information.

Now, I keep up-to-date on all things football, and I'm gearing up with my boys for the World Cup with knowledge and appreciation of what we are going to watch and experience together. I continually "research" just by checking my feeds as I normally do every day and having soccer information populate it on a regular basis.

How Does This Type of Research Work in School?

First, we have to acknowledge that we tend to do research in only one way (out of the many possible) in school. We often treat research as a JOB or TASK that students have to do in order to learn something.

This is where Googling, searching, and reading Wikipedia comes into play. Sometimes we get books on the topic as well.

And, if you are lucky, the content is not boring and dry. **But too often the content is just that: BORING.**

So, students believe research is boring. And they don't like it.

When students research only out of compliance, instead of curiosity, they lose the power of learning.

Second, we have to acknowledge that research can be fun and entertaining. We can watch great videos, read stories, listen to podcasts, and follow accounts on our favorite social media platforms.

It actually should be fun and exciting to learn in these ways if we have a purpose that extends beyond getting a grade for school.

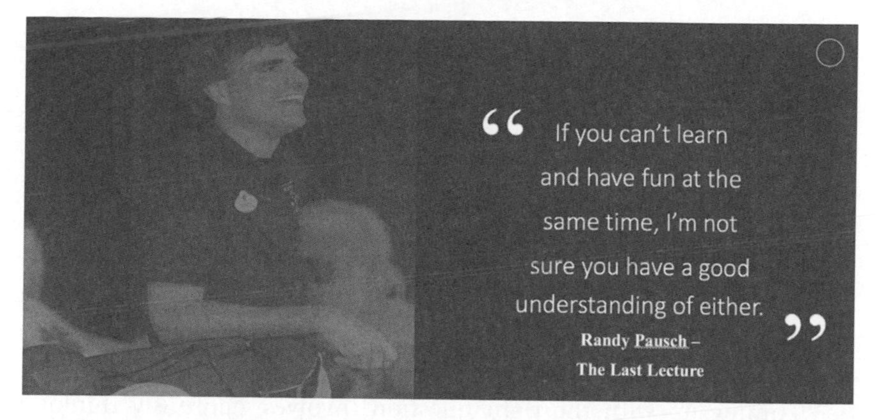

Third, we have to acknowledge that research can be both passive and active.

When my kids ask Amazon Alexa a question about something they are arguing about (Were George Washington and Alexander Hamilton really friends?), that is active research.

But they were also passively researching this same topic by listening to the Hamilton soundtrack on repeat for the past month and picking up the lyrics and story with each song.

This is why research can be so authentic in a project-based learning environment in our schools. It can be done in such a wide variety of ways that don't include searching journal articles or hopping on to Wikipedia as the only options.

Both journal articles and Wikipedia may be a part of the process in researching during PBL, but they'll never be the only options.

Inquiry as the Driver to Authentic Research in a Project-Based Environment

"The more we have familiarized ourselves with PBL, the more we have come to realize it is a series of best practices joined together."

—Ross Cooper and Erin Murphy in *Hacking Project Based Learning*

"What do you want to do today?"
"Where do you want to go for dinner?"
"What song should I put on?"
"Who said what?"

It seems all day long we are asking small questions. We ask questions in our family, at our workplace, in our schools, and online. There is no shortage of the questions we ask, or who we can ask them to, or what we ask them about.

Inquiry (which is the act of asking questions and researching) is not new. It's something we do constantly.

But when's the last time you asked a BIG question?

Dan Rothstein and Luz Santana, authors of the book *Make Just One Change: Teach Students to Ask Their Own Questions,* explain the importance of asking these questions:

Coming up with the right question involves vigorously thinking through the problem, investigating it from various angles, turning closed questions into open-ended ones and prioritizing which are the most important questions to get at the heart of the matter.

We've been underestimating how well our kids can think.

We see consistently that there are three outcomes. One is that students are more engaged. Second, they take more ownership, which for teachers, this is a huge thing. And the third outcome is they learn more—we see better quality work.

I'm fairly sure we would all gladly welcome more engagement, more ownership, and better quality work!

Asking these big questions takes time, mental energy, and a willingness to go beyond the daily grind of simple questions and answers. It's part mind-set, part opportunity.

As a teacher, I found myself wishing/wanting/hoping for my students to ask big questions and challenge themselves to solve big problems.

Yet I often did not encourage the mind-set or provide ample opportunity for them to do so in my classroom and in our school.

That changed the moment I gave ownership back to my students.

Our PBL experiences started with inquiry. They challenged students to ask big questions about big problems that mattered to them. And making that small tweak provided a huge spark in my class as they dove into research, brainstorming, ideating, prototyping, creating, and eventually launching their work to an audience.

But how do we begin to foster this inside our classroom? How can we get students to ask the right questions (and the big questions) instead of the daily small questions?

Asking the Right Questions

Phase Two of the Design Thinking LAUNCH Cycle is all about getting as many questions out in the open as possible. You can begin by telling students, "You know how teachers tell you that there are no stupid questions? Well, the only stupid question in a design project is 'Should I ask this question?' Because even a seemingly stupid question is a chance to learn."

You can explain that some of the best inventions began with a "stupid" question about combining two seemingly different ideas. A vague, half-baked idea is often the spark of innovation that challenges the status quo.

There's a certain bravery in asking questions—especially when questions seem silly or the kind that may challenge the presuppositions of the crowd. If a student asks a question that "everybody knows," that student is admitting ignorance. But here's the thing: sometimes it's the crowd that's ignorant.

Here are some quick ways to get students in the mind-set of asking big questions, and providing the opportunity for them to in class:

1. **Question everything.** Do this as a teacher as well; it will model what we want our students to do.
2. **Start with inquiry.** The idea is simple. Instead of starting a class period off with a question you created as a teacher, give that back to the students and their own inquiry.
3. **Give feedback on questions.** What makes a good question? A deep question? A big question?
4. **Practice it often.** Go beyond the LAUNCH Cycle to have students ask tons of questions. Put "inquiry" into every activity and lesson you do with students to build the culture of questioning.
5. **Spend more time playing.** Seriously. Wonder is both something we can promote in schools but also something we can allow—and the best way we allow this to happen is by promoting play.
6. **Provide support.** Some students have a really hard time with questioning strategies. In our book, *LAUNCH*, we provide you with a huge list of question stems to get students started.

7. **Embrace student choice.** Choice may start with a question, but it doesn't need to stop there. Embrace the idea that students can learn different types of content while mastering the same skills.
8. **Reduce the fear.** If students have had to spend most of their time getting the questions right, it can feel unnerving to be told that they can now ask their own questions.

Inquiry: It's Not a New Idea

There are those who believe Project-Based Learning, Genius Hour, and the LAUNCH Cycle are completely new ideas. But that's not true, far from it.

Inquiry has been driving the progress of humankind for centuries, just as it is today. This type of "inquiry-based learning" is really just *how we learn.*

Research is something that ALL of us do, ALL the time.

What's important is acknowledging research as a major part of the learning process. A major part that we have to allow for, make time for, support, and praise.

This quote from Anne Frank sums up the importance of inquiry and research perfectly:

> "Ever since I was a little girl and could barely talk, the word 'why' has lived and grown along with me… When I got older, I noticed that not all questions can be asked and that many whys can never be answered. As a result, I tried to work things out for myself by mulling over my own questions. And I came to the important discovery that questions which you either can't or shouldn't ask in public, or questions which you can't put into words, can easily be solved in your own head. **So the word 'why' not only taught me to ask, but also to think.** And thinking has never hurt anyone. On the contrary, it does us all a world of good."[17]

When I saw students in my class start with inquiry (instead of my teacher-directed questions), they were hooked on the one action that drives all learning: attention.

We tend to get students attention through necessity. Grades, due dates, and the process of schooling begs students to be compliant, follow the rules, and pay attention because they have to . . .

But what happens when students get tired of this game of school, or learn how to play it so well they aren't truly learning, but instead just going through the motions?

They aren't engaged. They aren't empowered. And they tend to stop asking questions, let alone big questions.

Well, that's where the idea of the "factory-model" of education comes into play. When students pay attention because they have to, and are compliant instead of engaged and empowered.

This, sadly, does not prepare our students to be the future movers and shakers we hope they will become.

And as Nobel Laureate Scientist Isidor Isaac Rabi explains, it can all be changed by focusing on questions:

> *My mother made me a scientist without ever intending to. Every other Jewish mother in Brooklyn would ask her child after school, "So? Did you learn anything today?" But not my mother.* **"Izzy," she would say, "did you ask a good question today?"** *That difference—asking good questions—made me become a scientist.*[18]

I first saw Joy Kirr write, "Inquiry. It's not a new idea."[19] The simplicity of those words spoke to me.

Innovation and creativity aren't always *new ideas.* Sometimes they are ideas and practices that have worked for centuries but presented in a form that empowers our students today.

Sometimes innovation and creativity have nothing to do with the latest technology, but instead, have everything to do with what we focus our time and attention on.

Let's bring it back to inquiry to start our projects and learning adventures. It works. It empowers. And it makes research as authentic as it is during our everyday lives.

Go to THEPBLPLAYBOOK.com for more resources, materials, and guiding questions about this chapter.

CHAPTER 7:

Assessing the PBL Experience

XOXXOXOOXO

My first full year of teaching was as an eighth-grade language arts teacher. It was my dream job at the time. I love the energy of middle school students, and I was still taller than most of them.

My situation was even better than expected because our MS teams had two language arts teachers, and I taught three 85-minute blocks, instead of five 40-minute blocks. Although this was more "time" teaching, it was fewer students per class and fewer students for my entire course load. It helped in grading especially (think of how long it takes to grade 130 essays versus 65 essays).

An added benefit that I did not see coming into the school year was how much extra time it would allow for me to understand and get to know my students. When you spend 80 minutes a day for 180 days you really get to know someone. I think of the connections elementary teachers can make with their students and know this bond is even stronger.

Midway through the school year, one of my students asked me if I'd share some of my own writing with them. I actually couldn't believe I had not done this yet. I had shared "examples" of papers that I crafted, but although these were original, they weren't authentic to the type of learning that I often did.

I told them I'd read something I wrote the next day, and it seemed like my students were more excited than they ever had been before, which is odd because we did a lot of fun activities throughout the school year.

That night I took out a memoir-type piece I had recently written about a friend passing away and how it changed my outlook on life. I wondered if this was "too heavy" for my eighth-grade students and then remembered that we all deal with loss and hopefully this could show how I grew since this tough time.

As I read aloud the memoir, "Three Bands on My Wrist," to my students, they sat and listened quietly. There was no technology involved. There was no particular instructional strategy being employed. It was just me, my words, and their attention.

After I finished they wanted to write their own memoirs and we began that same class period.

I can honestly say that some of their writing that week was the most inspired I have seen in all my years teaching. And it was their choice.

The next year I moved up to the HS English department, and two years later I was teaching tenth-grade English to many of the exact same students I had in eighth grade.

When they came into class I knew each student extremely well. I knew their background, family situations, interests, and learning tendencies. I was a bit more challenging as a tenth-grade teacher and that ruffled some feathers early on, but after that, we were able to get into some high-level types of activities because relationships were already built.

However, I did have one problem. Although I knew them personally, I was unable to see how much they had grown as learners over the past year. I had kept a few papers from that eighth-grade year, but not enough for every student. When I inquired with the ninth-grade teachers the problem was not resolved. There was no student work to look at.

This was another lightbulb moment in my young teaching career. Because we often start "fresh" with students we have never taught before, we tend to want to make our own judgments on their abilities from the first few assignments and assessments. It's from those first glances that we base our opinion and pedagogical strategies on.

Yet, with this group, I had taught them a year and a half ago. I knew them and what they could do but wasn't able to see growth in the past year.

That is when we made the decision to start digital portfolios in all my classes. I haven't stopped this practice since then, and highly recommend it not only for teachers but for entire departments and schools. It adds true choice to the assessment process.

Here's why.

What Can Students Do? The Portfolio Journey

We always want to know what our students understand and are able to do/apply. The problem is a multiple-choice assessment rarely ever provides that information. Yet these types of assessments are easy to grade, easy to distribute, and easy to reuse year after year with various tweaks. It is why many standardized assessments are multiple choice and why the SAT and ACT use this model for most of their questions.

What's worse, is that the idea of "data-driven" instruction is based on these various multiple-choice assessments and what they say about our students' abilities.

What kind of learning do these assessments promote?

1. Regurgitation and memorizing facts from study guides or stories
2. Only one right answer mentality
3. Rewards smart guessing and "playing the game"
4. Answers have to be "in your head"

The list could go on. As a former teacher who gave multiple-choice tests, and an SAT tutor for years who taught students how to take these tests, I'm embarrassed to say I once tied rigor and tough multiple-choice questions to deep learning.

I saw firsthand when I had that group of eighth-grade students again in tenth grade, what kind of information I can get from different forms of assessments. I was able to see how they did on standardized and district-level assessments, but unless their scores were off the charts (high or low), it didn't give me much info on what kind of learner they were or what kind of work they could produce.

What I can see by looking at student work is much different. A student portfolio shows me the following:

1. What the assignment/activity/assessment was and how the student approached it.
2. What kinds of personal experiences and biases they brought toward the assignment.
3. How well they demonstrated an understanding of the content.
4. How well they demonstrated their skill ability.
5. Usually some kind of reflection or metacognitive piece on what they did.
6. If they improved or not with the next piece in the portfolio.

The answer is obvious.

In fact, it's not only what every teacher wants to see from their former students, but it also makes it much easier to assess the growth of a student over the course of a semester or full-year class versus how much a final test or culminating project would show.

Portfolios helped me visually see where my students were struggling and where they were exceeding my expectations. Portfolios also allowed for student choice in the assessment process, which as we know lead to student engagement and ownership of their learning.

Choice in Demonstrating Ability and Understanding

Because we love multiple choice so much, let's take a quick quiz:

A student is trying to demonstrate their understanding of the rise and fall of Napoleon. In order to show what they know about this historic time period and the reasons behind Napoleon's rise and fall, they can be assessed through which activity:

1. *Writing a five-paragraph essay on the rise and fall of Napoleon*
2. *Creating an infographic on the rise and fall of Napoleon*
3. *Creating a political cartoon and rationale on the rise and fall of Napoleon*

4. *Creating a five-minute mini-documentary on the rise and fall of Napoleon*
5. *Creating a fictional serial-like podcast of interviews with key players in Napoleon's life*
6. *All of the above*

Don't you just love the "all of the above" option!

In any one of the above options, you could assess a student's understanding of the topic/situation and his or her ability to demonstrate the appropriate skill.

What's different about this scenario, is the choice provided to students allows them to "engage" in the material and claim some ownership over the assessment activity.

A Step-by-Step Process to Creating Choice-Based Assessments for PBL

If you are not familiar with the "Understanding by Design" framework, I highly recommend checking out this book by Grant Wiggins and Jay McTighe. In *UbD* (as it is commonly referred) you use the backward design process to create units.

For our purposes, this is extremely important. We want to create the assessment first, and then backward design the unit so that the content and activities students are doing matches the skills and standards covered on the assessment(s).

The first step is choosing your unit (this is most likely decided by your current curriculum).

The second step is choosing the skills you want your students to master and the applicable standards for the content and skills you are covering (hopefully this is also somewhat covered by your current curriculum).

For example, let's say the unit is all about "historical figures" in your state/area. You have a set curriculum and text to read (often an informational text such as a textbook). This current example can be for fifth grade. Jump onto the standards website and search for applicable standards for fifth grade "Reading: Informational Text" to find this:

CCSS.ELA-LITERACY.RI.5.1

Quote accurately from a text when explainin [illegible] explicitly and when drawing inferences from the tex [illegible]

CCSS.ELA-LITERACY.RI.5.2

Determine two or more main ideas of a text and [illegible] they are supported by key details; summarize the text.

CCSS.ELA-LITERACY.RI.5.3

Explain the relationships or interactions between two or more individuals, events, ideas, or concepts in a historical, scientific, or technical text based on specific information in the text.

The third step is now putting the pieces together for various assessments. The assessment must focus on similar content (historical figures), similar skills and standards (see the above three we will hit on), and have a similar rubric for grading.

Let's talk about the rubric for a moment. Here's where many teachers get stuck . . . and it takes a long time to create. And who has that much time!?

Lucky for all of us there are some very easy and efficient ways to create standards-based rubrics online. My favorite tool is essaytagger .com/commoncore.

It took me less than five minutes to create this sample rubric based on our example standards:

Example Common Core Rubric (LBC)
Common Core-aligned rubric (5th Grade)
shared by Created by A.J. Juliani
www.EssayTagger.com/rubric?code=

	Below 5th *(weakest)*	Beginning	Emerging	Proficient	Above 5th *(strongest)*
Quote Text in Explanations (¶) *paragraph-level* Reading: Informational Text: RI.5.1					
Quote Text in Inferences *sentence-level* Reading: Informational Text: RI.5.1					
Determine Main Ideas (¶) *paragraph-level* Reading: Informational Text: RI.5.2					
Key Detail Support *whole document* Reading: Informational Text: RI.5.2					
Summarize Text *whole document* Reading: Informational Text: RI.5.2					
Explain Relationships or Interactions (¶) *paragraph-level* Reading: Informational Text: RI.5.3					

What's nice about EssayTagger is the ability to personalize and change all of the categories above in the top row. The categories down the side are straight from the standards and skills we pulled for this unit.

Ask yourself after creating the rubric, "Can this work for various types of assessments for this unit?"

If the answer is "Yes," then you've got a rubric to work with. If the answer is still "No," you'll have to either create a new rubric or revisit Step #2 for some clarity.

The fourth step is allowing your students to choose their preferred assessment or create their own assessment. As we discussed in my last article, choice empowers students and engages them in the material.

I used to have a bank of various assessment types that my students could look through and choose the assessment that best fit their personality, interests, and learning styles. However, over time more and more students started to use the first option on that list: make your own assessment.

Some of the assessment ideas that came from students include the following:

- "I want to make a Saturday Night Live parody skit around this topic, and poke fun at the way it was handled in a historical sense."
- "I want to conduct an in-depth interview with the author, where my friend will play the role of the author, and we'll get into a heated argument."
- "I want to create a flip-book-style comic to show the character's story arc."

This list could go on. Students are much more creative in their assessment ideas than I ever could be!

The fifth step is conferencing with students on their plan. You'll want to make sure students understand the following:

- What the end-goal is for this assessment
- How they are being assessed (look at the rubric together)
- What the expectations are for their work

- What a time line looks like for their assessment
- An action plan of how they are going to get it finished

This is one of the most important pieces of allowing choice in assessment. A traditional assessment dictates all of the terms listed above. You know when the test date is, what type of content is going to be on the test, how much each question is worth, when the study guide needs to be completed, etc. . . .

Here, the short conference serves as a guiding plan for completing the choice-based assessment, and demonstrating a high level of understanding.

My students always felt better after this mini-conference because the goals, outcomes, and steps were clearly laid out in front of them, as well as how they would be ultimately assessed on their project.

The sixth step is digitizing the project and sharing it with the class and in their portfolio. Regardless of what assessment type students choose, they need to create a digital record of this assessment to put in their online portfolio. This is easy to do if the work was done on a digital device, but if it was not, you'll need to take pictures (or video recordings) to upload to the portfolio.

Teachers ask me all the time what they should use for student digital portfolios. I'd first recommend using a platform that your school is already using (Google Apps for Education, Microsoft 365, or Apple options).

By starting out with a simple Google Drive (or SkyDrive) folder, you can eventually give the students a choice down the road of what platform they want to create their digital portfolio so they can share it with the world. Here is where students will make their own websites using Wordpress.com, Weebly.com, Wix.com, Squarespace.com, and many more options.

The seventh step is grading the assessment (teacher grade and student grade). A big piece of this type of assessment is to have students grade themselves using the rubric. They were fully aware (from the earlier conference) what was expected and how their work demonstrates understanding. The act of reflecting and grading themselves makes this all the more transparent.

After students grade themselves, I would look at the rubric and their assessment to see if I had different thoughts on what was demonstrated. Interestingly, most of my students were incredibly honest throughout this process and were harder on themselves than I might have been when grading them.

If the student's grade and my grade were completely off base, then I would have another short conference to talk about expectations and outcomes for this assessment so we could get on the same page.

The eighth step is actually assessing the portfolio itself. At the end of the unit, marking period, semester, or year, it's important to assess the overall work of the student in their portfolio. Art teachers have been doing this for years, and more and more colleges are requesting to see real student work as part of the admission process.

To make a real-world connection (and I sometimes hate that phrase), think of your students' digital portfolios as the first steps in their academic resume, but also in crafting their personal brand.

The choices they make in what the create/make/do for assessments, will directly impact the choices they make in their career and life path. If they do not document this journey, then it will be hard to reflect on why they made choices and what they have learned along the way.

Go to THEPBLPLAYBOOK.com for more resources, materials, and guiding questions about this chapter.

PART 2:
PBL in Action across the Grades and Subjects

The following chapters are the "meat" of this book. In each chapter you will find stories of real projects happening in real classrooms around the world. In many books these types of resources are left for the end of the book. Often they are placed in the appendix section as an add-on to the actual book.

Not in *The PBL Playbook*.

The goal of this book is to give you actionable ideas and projects that you can implement in your class and school immediately.

Maybe you won't implement the actual projects shared in the following chapters, but it just might inspire you to create your own PBL unit and experience for your students.

CHAPTER 8:

PBL Making an Impact

XOXXOXOOXO

Eat your heart out, Rembrandt.
pic.twitter.com/hN42zJ3NPJ
—Harriett Gilbert (@HarriettSG)
December 7, 2014

This photo went viral a few years ago, as people from around the world shared how it was a "reflection" of our current generation and society. They wanted this photo (as with the recent video from Simon Sinek) to support their own beliefs about younger generations who seem to have their heads buried in a phone/screen all day long.

But what was really happening?

The photo on the next page was shared by literary translator Lammie Oostenbrink who explained: "There's another picture of the same group of kids, totally mesmerized by one of his portraits.

"The kids used the iPhones as part of the tour of the museum. Special app.... The interpretation of the photo was just wrong. I tried to correct it."

@wijdopenogen @PieterSteinz @rijksmuseum Hi, I was also there this afternoon. Saw this breathless listening: pic.twitter.com/wfjC5LqXiD
—Jan Postma (@j_postma) November 27, 2014

And here is her tweet, translated:

Over and over again, our assumptions around the current generation and their views on technology, learning, and everything else are construed by context.

While this example can be played out in malls, parks, subways, and classrooms around the world, there is a bigger piece to the context discussion that I failed to acknowledge as a teacher and now as a school leader.

Without context, you only have one view of the situation. With context, you can see not only the situation as a clear picture but also how circumstances have impacted that situation.

This happens often in our learning discussions, and I've seen it more and more at all levels of the education system.

- Administrators make decisions about teachers, curriculum, and policies without understanding the full context.
- Students make decisions about teachers, assignments, projects without understanding the full context.
- Parents make decisions about teachers, administrators, and schools without understanding the full context.
- Teachers make decisions about students without understanding the full context.

The list could go on, and I have seen it myself, especially in regards to research on best practices.

I once read a study about the marshmallow test. I'm sure many of you have heard about the marshmallow test as well. It can be paraphrased here:

> *In the original Stanford marshmallow experiment, children were given one marshmallow. They could eat the marshmallow right away; or, if they waited fifteen minutes for the experimenter to return without eating the marshmallow, they'd get a second marshmallow. Even more interestingly, in follow-up studies two decades later, the children who waited longer for the second marshmallow, that is, showed delayed gratification, had higher SAT scores, school performance, and even improved body mass index. This is normally interpreted as indicating the importance of self-control and delayed gratification for life success.*

I believed this study showed everything we needed to know about *grit* and why it was so important for our kids to have a growth mind-set. I watched Angela Duckworth's TED Talk on the subject and shared it with everyone I knew in education. Although I was preaching growth mind-set, my mind was "fixed" on this study without thinking about the context.

But as it tends to do, the context made me rethink things:

In a new variant of the marshmallow experiment entitled "Rational Snacking," Celeste Kidd, Holly Palmeri, and Richard N. Aslin from the University of Rochester gave the children similar tests with a **new context.**

The researchers put the children into two groups and asked them to perform art projects. Children in the first group each received small box of used crayons, and were told that if they could wait, the researcher would bring them more and better art supplies. However, after three minutes, the adult returned and told the child they had made a mistake, and there were no more art supplies so they'd have to use the original crayons.

Children in the second group went through the same routine except for this time the adult fulfilled their promises, bringing the children more and better art supplies

Group 1 was told to wait and lied to. Group 2 was told to wait and was rewarded for their patience.

Now for the next iteration, the adult now gave the children in the first group a single sticker and told the child that if they waited, the adult would bring them more stickers to use. Again the adult came back and said there were no stickers.

Children in the second group did the same routine with stickers and were rewarded for their patience again.

It wasn't until after these two routines with the art supplies and the stickers that the researchers finally did repeated the classic marshmallow test with both groups.

Here's what happened:

> *The results demonstrated children were a lot more rational than we might have thought. Of the 14 children in group 1, who had been shown that the experimenters were unreliable adults, 13 of them ate the first marshmallow. Eight of the 14 children in the reliable adult group, waited out the fifteen minutes. On average children in unreliable group 1 waited only 3 minutes, and those in reliable group 2 waited 12 minutes.*[20]

I took the first marshmallow test on face value. I didn't think about what the various experiences were like in their households growing up. I didn't consider what context of life they had lived versus the other kids in the experiment.

Context changes everything.

And if we don't have context, we can be led to believe that a group of students working on an app to research art in a museum are instead not paying attention and sucked into their phones.

If we don't have context we can believe that studies, and research, and best practices work for all students, regardless of what context they are bringing with them into school.

I've been reminded too many times by my own inability to see the context of a situation that this is an integral piece of learning conversations.

Bring multiple minds, perspectives, and people to the table when talking about students, curriculum, technology, and best practices in our learning environments.

If we don't, we run the risk of missing the big picture, and believing a one-sided view of a situation.

In each of the projects shared in this chapter, context plays an important piece in the learning puzzle. These teachers and students are solving big problems, with a real impact on the world around them. Their view of the issue is helped by the context of their situation.

Katherine Johnson

Mentor High School: Teacher
10 years of teaching experience
Causes Worth Fighting For

In Katherine Johnson's "Causes Worth Fighting For" project, students select a societal issue (locally or globally) that is important to them and strive to become agents of change, to make an impact on improving their selected topic in some way. In some cases, projects are research intensive with the goal of educating others. In other cases, projects are more hands-on, requiring careful planning and execution. There is quite a bit of choice in this project and a high level of personal accountability. Katherine's goal is to put students in situations where they have to practice communication skills that many are under equipped for handling when they advance to postsecondary school, such as making a simple phone call, scheduling an appointment with a contact, writing a professional e-mail, and persevering when they hit dead ends. Some of their projects are instant success stories, but most of her students hit several roadblocks along the way. Katherine's goal is to show them that there is much to be learned through failure and they should never give up.

This unit was created specifically as a result of a push for PBL in Katherine's district. She wanted somcthing that both her and her students could walk away feeling good about. She wanted something that would provide them all with a unique and authentic experience. Katherine's ideas were constructed after several professional development sessions on PBL.

Katherine's students are assessed using the following: summative assessment through formal writing and reflection, summative assessment through formal presentation of materials in a final showcase conducted in April (community members are invited to the final project exposition where students present their projects), formative assessments over the course of the project through work logs, and also formative assessments through weekly meetings with students.

The rapport Katherine has built with her students over the last two years has been incomparable to years past. Her students all pick topics that are deeply meaningful to them. She gets to hear their story (the good and the bad) and they get to tell it, and be proud of it. Some are deeper than others, but they all have walked away with a true sense of pride in their work. The gratitude they have shown at the project completion speaks volumes. Many started off feeling like this project was just like any other. The skills and experience they walk away with though, is unlike anything many have experienced before. Students have picked projects that they plan to study further in college. Students have picked projects that have allowed them to showcase skills that they have that would otherwise not be displayed and they get to link that to charitable causes. This has been refreshing to Katherine because what they choose is at the core of who they are.

The following is a link to the slide show Katherine created for the most recent years' project. It showcases some great projects from that year. https://docs.google.com/presentation/d/1NKlpZHaIsrEhyPbM7rfyPzCYdAwjqr_pfDrte0S6YBI/edit?usp=sharing.

Katherine also likes to add that she had a number of student projects that did indeed fail which Katherine feels is equally, if not more, valuable than a successful project. Part of what she wants to teach her students is that there is so much to be learned through failure and that in the real world, you have to pick up and try again when something doesn't go your way the first time around. Even though their projects may have failed, the effort that they put into them is what's important.

Katherine's particular project's purpose was to give students real-world experience in research, writing, and communication skills. Her students were given freedom to explore whatever they wanted in whatever field they were interested in, as long as they were meeting the ELA standards (which wasn't hard to do in this project). The biggest struggle Katherine faced was from a small group of teachers in a different subject area who were extremely critical of her work, not fully understanding the project and ELA standards she was addressing. She did her best to explain to them the nature of the project and why her students were doing things that were not "English" projects. Ultimately, Katherine isn't sure they wanted to hear anything about it. She did take this as an opportunity to learn and contacted staff members at the start of this year's project with a brief explanation of what students were doing and to contact her if they'd like to be involved and/or learn more.

Melissa Dyas

Alvey Elementary, Prince William County Schools, VA, 5th-grade teacher
16 years of teaching experience
Mission: Planet Z

Melissa Dyas sparks an interest in her students by telling them that a distant planet has recently been discovered that is similar to Earth and ideal for colonizing. They will work in teams of a captain, geologist, farmer, and engineer to learn as much about Earth's resources as possible, engineering designs and energy sources, and farming techniques. Experiencing a modern-day journey like the courageous settlers of the Midwest, this adventure will establish a new frontier for pioneers. Detailed questions each person in the team will need to ask themselves can be found here: https://drive.google

.com/file/d/18HQOX6ATtTdTY9WSzzCiaEO6TgcQP7LB/view?usp=sharing.

This is a two-month endeavor in which most of the day is dedicated toward this project. Almost every subject is integrated as well as fourth-grade science standards which are tested in fifth grade. The integration is natural. Melissa and her students study and make connections between weather phenomena, climates, regions, Earth's rotation, and seasons. They study rock types, locations, and uses. They discuss natural, renewable, and nonrenewable resources as well as alternative forms of energy. They discuss human impact, both negative and positive. They make observations and inferences, and always connect back to why this knowledge would be useful in colonizing a new planet. In social studies, they study regions and in learning about the Midwest, discuss early settlers in the pioneering days, using resources around them and farming techniques. They take an abundance of notes, journal their plans, and prepare for the trip to the unknown. Truly students do not know what they will be experiencing.

The "trip" is a one-day culmination of this project where the skills are put to use. Melissa spends a long weekend creating a planet in an empty classroom in her building. She designs the room so students will have much to discover: rocks, fossils, plants, sand, soil, water (fresh and salt), an active volcano, and signs of animal life (tracks, droppings). Students pack a bag of supplies to take with them, and they travel to this new planet still with no idea of what to expect. When they arrive, each team has a journal (like Lewis & Clark), and they explore their surroundings. They identify as much as they can, make inferences about this new environment, and eventually choose a place to settle. They take advantage of the resources on the planet, including a large forest (donated boxes) and build a shelter large enough for their team. Then they must plant crops to begin farming, begin to set up and use alternative energy sources (solar power, hydropower, water filters, etc.), and establish a colony on this new planet. Their final task is to create a video broadcast to be sent back to the people of Earth (parents, to be watched the next day in class, clip for morning announcements, etc.) highlighting their discoveries and settlement on Planet Z. Throughout the entire day, Melissa is discussing all their observations and choices with them.

She also invites other teachers and administrative personnel to visit and interview students.

Students know the information at a much more meaningful level because they are thinking critically and applying so many different ideas in an authentic and natural way. They are excited to learn and prepare for the mission because they truly don't know what to expect.

Melissa assesses their knowledge throughout the project with activities that have them demonstrate both their understanding and their application. She also learns a lot about what they know based on her interviews and discussions with them during the day of the "trip." It's essentially a six-hour test of skills.

Melissa is constantly amazed at what she's seen students think of. She's seen students create homemade functional water filters. Another group used a circuit kit to build a radio system to try to signal back to Earth. She's seen students build solar panels and plant crops/seeds that later "sprouted" as they replaced crops with pipe cleaners. She once saw a very quiet student make a medical kit using special rocks and shells she collected around the land and then pretending to treat people in need. I've seen students get into live video recordings and act as news reporters showing all different features of the new planet. When "night" descends upon the new planet, all of the students suddenly start pretending to be wild animals and truly get into the creative spirit and role-play of the project. Working in teams of four, there are always some students who just jump into leadership and some quiet workers who really just work hard contributing to their teams. Melissa didn't expect or anticipate any of those creations or ideas, but allowing the students to guide the project and being open to following their journey led her to so many more experiences and connections.

Now that Melissa is so comfortable with the curriculum and knows the connections between content areas and having the ability to integrate larger-scale activities throughout the day, she finds that she is able to make more in-depth, meaningful, and authentic experiences. Students are more motivated to learn, more active in the learning process, and usually end up covering way more than the curriculum actually requires. Students also learn better communication and teamwork skills, organization, problem-solving, and time management in the process of PBL than in anything that would been planned in a traditional setting.

The obvious struggle with this PBL project is the amount of time and curriculum it encompasses as well as preparing students for the unknown. Melissa spends about six weeks and integrates in just about every subject area. Maintaining momentum and excitement, especially when the students don't actually know what they're preparing for, is sometimes hard. She doesn't want to give them information about the "big trip" event so it's a lot of discussions of "how would this information help you . . . ?" or "why might this be important to know?" The other challenge is physically setting up the space for this one. It takes several hours to transform a room into another planet. Melissa would like to someday have real water for sampling and the illusion of water (blue plastic tablecloths) plus an active volcano, forest, rocks correctly placed, plants, signs of animal life, and the like.

Melissa's advice regarding PBL is to choose an area of the curriculum that you are very comfortable and confident in first. Think of an authentic application/experience for the skills, and a way to share that knowledge outside of your classroom. Be prepared that the path of knowledge will stray far from the traditional line that you are used to. If students get too far off track, include some mini-lessons to fit in the must-know information, but continually tie in the project goal and how this new information will/could fit into it. Highlight the important and innovative ideas that groups come up with, and other groups will follow their example (without you even telling them to). Relax and just go with it—enjoy the students and their learning.

Darren Withey

Legend High School (EDGE Academy) teacher/mentor
18 years of teaching experience
Change Campaign

For the past fifteen years, Darren Withey's students have gotten their vocabulary list from their book. There was zero interaction among other curriculums, students had no buy-in to the lesson, and there was a hypothetical end assessment and not much result.

This project is combined with humanities, English, Spanish, and technology. Spanish students are choosing their vocabulary unit and will create a Public Service Announcement in Spanish for a 30-second English/Spanish announcement to make a local change in their community. Humanities will be doing the humans explore, think, lead, and create and be able to link that to their English and Spanish speech. English will be working with Darren in prepping the students for oral presentation skills, and technology will be working on putting together a business dashboard with students' surveys.

Everything Darren does is based on PBL. The students have created their "I can" statements to give them specific direction, each day they are working toward their individual outcome and their PSA announcement that will be recorded and uploaded to their ePortfolio. Darren has afternoon workshops that will deal with the "Content" portion of what they need to know and how to speak. Students will then add their workshop sessions to their PSA announcement. By working with other content areas, all the teachers are able to touch base one on one with students, see their progress, and give them constant feedback. This produces more accountability from each student. Each student can speak specifically to what they are learning and what they need to be working on each and every day. Their application from workshops to projects coincides wonderfully, and the relationships built among mentor and student allows for each student to know they can approach mentors/teachers with problems and questions.

The end result will be their PSA announcement, and their speaking will be assessed on that. There are four checking points throughout this process. Weekly speaking assessments will be assessed, and each student will receive feedback from Darren to progress them in the right direction. They will also be working on Spanish debates with the assistance of English and teaching the persuasive opinion approach to the end project.

Due to Darren's research for his dissertation and how colleges and businesses are moving toward the PBL model, his focus has turned to trying to help other teachers move toward individual student ideas and working toward a project that the students "own." He has shifted toward a more individual focus for learning.

Zander Lyvers

American International School, Hong Kong
6 years of teaching experience
Israel/ Palestine Subway Wars

When Zander Lyvers taught in NYC, the *NY Times* published a story about a physical altercation that had erupted in a midtown subway station. A pro-Palestinian and pro-Israeli activist had clashed over a controversial advertisement that stated, "In a War between the Civilized Man and the Savage, Support the Civilized Man. Support Israel. Defeat Jihad." As an entry event, Zander and his students watched the altercation on YouTube, but this set up the driving question, "How can we make an advertisement that promotes understanding instead of violence?" To do this, students joined into groups and researched the history of the issue from the creation of the Jewish diaspora to the current state of the conflict. After students researched, they began to come up with a visual concept for their advertisement for the NYC MTA subway system. Students had to write an ad proposal based on their research and creative vision by writing collaboratively about the target audience, the objective of the ad, and then explaining the history behind their symbolic choices. Zander was able to bring in two experts for this project. His graphic design friend, Mckenna, worked at an advertising firm and was able to give students feedback on their ads. He also reached out to a nonprofit organization called OneVoice, which is a group that promotes peace between Palestinians and Israelis. During the exhibition, a representative from OneVoice was able to come in and give students feedback on their projects after sharing her recent trip to the region. She also posted an article on the OneVoice blog discussing the projects, which really elevated the authenticity of the project: https://www.onevoicemovement.org/news/facebookview/in-queens-high-school-students-create-ads-for-israeli-palestinian-peace.

Students were able to practice their research skills and collaborate to synthesize information and create a visual concept that helps promote understanding. Students were able to discuss big questions around identity, nationality, and religious conflict by using the content of the Arab-Israeli conflict as evidence for their arguments.

This was Zander's first successful PBL unit from his first year of teaching in 2013. He has since taught this unit two more times. Zander has now used this unit to better personalize education for each student, so he teaches this in more of an asynchronous way. Students now complete tasks asynchronously before joining into groups and creating the project. For this project Zander mainly used formative assessments when he had check-ins about the students' research logs, and finally he had students write a thematic essay about the Israeli-Palestinian conflict after the exhibition of the projects.

This is a project that allows students who are learning English to master the content in a basic way while learning research and informational writing skills. Students whose skill levels are medium to high typically go down a rabbit hole and learn so much more about the Arab-Israeli conflict than most American adults probably know. Student collaboration and engagement increased when Zander first taught it because it was based on an issue that had happened in the NYC subway, which helped bridge the gap between local and global issues.

Looking back to Zander's past, he was hired to teach in a PBL school in NYC before he even knew what PBL was (The Young Women's Leadership School of Astoria). The principal had a very clear vision of incorporating PBL into the class, despite having to teach to the content-heavy regents tests. Ever since then Zander has spread the gospel of PBL to his current colleagues in Hong Kong and has continued to give presentations on the methodology.

James Bruegenhemke

Wentzville School District—Teacher
13 years of teaching experience
Food Allergy and Anaphylactic Shock Education/Prevention

James Bruegenhemke's driving force question: "How can we reduce the risk of any food allergy or peanut allergic reaction attack in Rm 516, at Boone Trail Elementary, or anywhere within the Wentzville School District?"

James's students researched to educate themselves about food allergies and anaphylactic shock risk and preventions. Through their education, students shared their stories, wrote persuasive essays, created infographic posters, were trained how to read labels, had EpiPen training, and created PSA videos. Students then hosted a Food Allergy/Anaphylactic Shock Summit to educate others. James says that student work and accountability increased greatly due to the understanding that their work was going public to be shared with others. James implemented individual student assessments of the work throughout the project and peer/group evaluations at the end of the project. An example of those assessments is seen here.

PSA Components	5	4	3	2	1
Storyboard The storyboard describes the overall message of the PSA from beginning, middle to end. Each slide has a focused message with an image, sketch, graphic or description of filming idea.					
Creativity The message is told in unexpected or novel ways. Elements in the message are woven together with insight and imagination grabbing the attention of the intended audience.					
Tag Line The message is clear and concise. A single thought or phrase within the PSA summarizes the entire message.					
Social Benefit The ideas shown have an application to the lives of the targeted audience. The PSA is one that will motivate change to improve the targeted audience's community in a meaningful way.					
Facts The message is based on accurate and verifiable information. Opinion or bias expressed is based in and supported by fact. Source information has been verified and documented.					
Written Work All deadlines are met. Pitch, Glossary, Storyboard, shot list, and script have been turned in on time before working with a group to create a group PSA video.					

Dr. Ruchi Gupta MD MPH and her Northwestern University Researcher's SMHRT (Student Media-Based Health Research Team) were instrumental in this project. They invited James and his class to pilot their SMHRT curriculum. After much research, many subject-matter-expert presentations, and determination, James's class rose to the challenge and exceeded all expectations to become food allergy experts. His class made food allergy glossaries, posters, storyboards, PSA videos, persuasive essays, and presentations. As his class became experts, they found a passion, a need, and a desire to share their knowledge and teach others about anaphylactic shock and food allergy awareness. Upon completion of this lesson, Dr. Gupta and her SMHRT team invited his students to include their PSA videos in their SMHRT Curriculum that will be shared with other students nationwide.

There were many successes and some failures that came to life during this PBL lesson. Many students thrived and shined with much success in learning in a new, exciting but challenging way, while some students struggled with some frustrations of not learning in the traditionally structured classroom. Many of James's gains were not only his students' curriculum-based lessons, but more importantly were the gains exceeded in the twenty-first-century skills of problem-solving, creativity, analytic thinking, collaboration, and communication.

James's biggest success that made him most proud was not in his students' classroom lessons or twenty-first-century skills but was in his student for whom this lesson was built around. Ryan is his ten-year-old student with severe peanut allergies who typically relied on others to be his advocate for his condition. He relied on his doctor, mom, school nurse, and teachers to assure him he was safe within the classroom, but after our four-week food-allergies lesson, Ryan's confidence, independence, and self-advocacy to care for himself turned him into a new, much more relaxed and confident student within the classroom and entire school. After the PBL lesson, his doctor recognized his growth and confidence so much to the point that he suggested Ryan to participate in a peanut allergy patch study that will hopefully someday decrease his chances of a possible anaphylactic shock peanut allergy episode and possibly improve his condition.

Since using PBL in his classroom, James has a new perspective of education and his job as an educator. In his thirteen years of teaching, he is amazed at how much teaching and students have changed in a short amount of time. Students are changing, thus teachers must change to meet the needs of their students. PBL engages and excites students, and they don't even realize their work is improving; they enjoy being in the classroom. In regards to his teaching career, James not only teaches students but also enjoys sharing his experiences of PBL with other educators. He conducts learning labs, presented at professional development events and conferences about his successes in PBL to encourage other educators to give it a try.

Bryan Kuhlman and Claudia Litz

Mentor High School Intervention Specialist and General Education Science Teacher
4 and 32 years of teaching experience, respectively
Amazing Amusement Park Attractions

Claudia Litz had been a teacher with twenty-eight years of teaching experience in the same school district when that district first introduced PBL. She said to her coteacher, Bryan Kuhlman, "this is what I had been doing years ago!" They were immediately dedicated to PBL. They spent 175 hours that following summer and reshaped the entire teaching layout and plan for their first semester class. This planning took a while due to the process of adding station rotations to save some class days and changing the daily experiences and activities to better match the theme and putting together their Amazing Amusement Park Attraction PBL. This is a semester-long PBL unit that Bryan and Claudia say covers the physics portion of the ninth-grade physical science course. These topics include forces and motion, energy, electricity, waves, light and sound, and engineering and design.

Blended learning and station rotations, incorporating mini labs and experiments along with rubrics and checkpoints to make sure students are staying on track and meeting deadlines are all incorporated. The team also did one-on-one interviews with the students for the first two checkpoints to make sure the students were on the right track and took it seriously. Also, Bryan and Claudia use peer evaluations and gallery walks for the students to give each other input and feedback on their PBL.

A big part of the PBL was making sure it looked and felt authentic for the students and they wanted the community to be involved on some level. The team had an engineer come in a few times to go through each of the students' projects with them so he could give them direct feedback and help with some of the creation ideas. This really helped the students get to that next level of engagement and authenticity.

Bryan and Claudia teach a total of 125 students a semester in physical science. Before the PBL was included in their teachings, they, on an average, had six to seven students fail a semester. Since embedding the PBL into the curriculum, they are now down to one student failing a semester for each of the last two years. Students are retaining knowledge longer, which is evident by them being able to reference content from the first semester. Along with all the academic gains, Bryan and Claudia have seen much improvement in their students' soft skills including eye contact when speaking to others, more confidence in themselves when they present and talk about the content, their persistence when overcoming obstacles, and the way they maintain a positive attitude throughout the PBL due to student choice.

In one of their cotaught classes, Bryan and Claudia had a set of twins who got added to their class after the semester started because they were failing in another teacher's physical science class. Their reading levels were at the first and second grade. Because the PBL groups had already started, the twins worked in a group by themselves which they were very pleased with! This also worked well based on what Bryan and Claudia knew about them. They ended up learning quite a lot of content and doing a great job on their project. Because the PBL was embedded in their daily work (and vice versa), these two students went from an F with a different teacher to a C– and a C+ from Bryan and Claudia.

Bryan and Claudia held an evening exhibition open to the community and so many of the comments they heard revolved around how well the students knew their content and how strong their soft skills were—communicating and maintaining eye contact, the way they presented their project and themselves (everyone dressed up), the technology involved, and their ability to collaborate and explain the difference between collaborative learning and cooperative learning.

This teaching duo is very aware that their students have become more engaged in their learning and have shown a greater retention of more information. They have become more independent learners and try to figure out things themselves or collaborate with their peers to find a solution to their problem. If the educational pendulum does not swing back the other way, being the teacher in the classroom will remain more fun and creative. This style of teaching will keep, and possibly attract, more teachers into the profession.

Go to THEPBLPLAYBOOK.com for more resources, materials, and guiding questions about this chapter.

CHAPTER 9:

Little Learners, Big Ideas

XOXXOXOOXO

To be honest, I was lost. Elementary teaching was something so new to me when I took a job years ago as a K-12 technology staff developer.

I taught middle school. I taught high school. I had written curriculum for those levels and connected with many educators who teach at those levels, learning so much along the way.

So, what did I do with this new scary K-5 area? I reached out online. I found teachers who were sharing what they were doing in their classes through blogs and social media and podcasts.

I listened and learned from teachers in my own district. I watched them teach, saw how the students learned, and soaked in the best practices that were all around me.

What I realized that first year in a K-12 role is that innovation in an elementary school revolves around many of the same concepts and topics as the secondary levels, but it's doesn't always look the same.

One of the biggest misconceptions we have with innovation in education is that technology has to be present. Technology doesn't necessarily lead to innovation.

Instead, technology often allows for new ways of teaching and learning, but only if used for the right purpose. This chapter focuses on real elementary teachers doing Project-Based Learning with kids of all ages in a variety of subject and cross-curricular approaches. Dive in and be inspired by these little learners with great big ideas and creative projects!

Ashleigh Anderson

Micro Elementary in North Carolina, 1st-grade teacher
6 years of teaching experience
We Bought a Zoo

When Ashleigh Anderson student-taught just a few years ago, lecturing was the norm and she was not a fan. Ashley was introduced to PBL during her second year of teaching, and she now feels passionate about teaching. She explains that with PBL she has two steps throughout the unit. The first one involves the student work, and the second is the students collaborating together.

Ashleigh's first-grade class "bought a zoo" and named it together. Each zookeeper was in charge of selecting one animal for the zoo, researching the animal, and convincing the rest of the class that they should have this animal. They were in charge of preparing a habitat for their animal and providing educational resources for visitors. Ashleigh assembled a long list of standards this unit was fulfilling. Just to name a few:

- 1.L.1 Understand characteristics of various environments and behaviors of humans that enable plants and animals to survive.
- 1.L.1.1 Recognize that plants and animals need air, water, light (plants only), space, food, and shelter and that these may be found in their environment.
- 1.L.1.2 Give examples of how the needs of different plants and animals can be met by their environments in North Carolina or different places throughout the world.
- RI.1.5 Know and use various text features (e.g., headings, tables of contents, glossaries, electronic menus, icons) to locate key facts or information in a text.

Individual student work involved creating a book about their animal to use when they presented to the group to advocate for their animal to earn a position in the zoo. They also created an animal advertisement to convince the other "zookeepers" to bring this animal to the zoo. During the group work, the zoo was divided into different ecosystems, and the children collaborated together to decide which animals would be featured in that ecosystem. They then worked together to create that habitat and animal together.

Ashleigh testifies that the impact of Project-Based Learning is far greater than any other way she has ever taught. Her students' learning is personalized to their needs and wants. It is about the student learning and engaging about they want to learn. Yes, it surrounds a topic, but their choices of what to do with the information is endless. The *learning* is endless. There isn't an endpoint. What better educational practice can you offer a struggling student? Your job as a teacher is to set every student up to succeed. No matter a child's background, the impact is greater with this practice. Project-Based Learning allows a hands-on approach that offers a time to investigate and respond to a complex question. Students are learning at their own pace, and Ashleigh encourages them as they do.

Ashleigh practices checkpoints throughout her projects to ensure the student learning. She uses self-made rubrics or other rubrics that she has already found and tweaks them to make them her own. Ashleigh's favorite quote that sums up education is by poet Arthur O'Shaunessy, "We are the music-makers and we are the dreamers of dreams." Ashleigh realizes that she helps mold the minds that dream their own dreams and help those march to the beat of their own drum. When people think of classrooms, they envision students sitting in desks quietly, completing their worksheets. You walk into Ashleigh's classroom and you see the complete opposite. Construction paper covers the floor, boxes are cut up, and crayons are scattered about. The noise is loud, but if you listen, it's productive.

Ashleigh strongly believes that inquiry-based learning is imperative for schools today. Careers are quickly changing in society, and new jobs are being created every day. Problem-Based Learning helps students adapt and learn all of the twenty-first-century skills they will need when they start their career. They learn to cooperate and collaborate because they are working in teams to solve a problem. They can communicate and work through their differences without arguing to build strong communication skills. This takes a lot of practice, but it sets them up to understand how to work through problems later in life with others.

Ashleigh took out the desks and replaced them with tables this year to really help promote more collaboration.

Project-Based Learning has given her students a chance to travel the globe and experience things that they never could sitting in a desk in North Carolina. Ashleigh will admit that with PBL you will always fail, but it's the great teachers that come up with a different plan and try again. Ashleigh personally has had times where she felt defeated and got upset that the projects did not work out the way she wanted them to. But it's the moments when her students can tell you exactly what they learned and the smiles on their faces that are priceless.

Lisa Mitchell: Grade-2 teacher and curriculum coordinator

Barbara Reade: Grade-2 teacher

12 years and 26 years of teaching experience
Hillfield Strathallan College, Hamilton, Ontario
PBL Project: The Mouse Library

Lisa Mitchell attended a PBL conference held at Hillfield Strathallan College. She was eager to get back to school and discuss what she had learned with her teaching partner, Barbara Reade. They were both super excited to try this innovative approach to learning.

Lisa wrote a blog post with numerous details about this project. You can find it here: http://www.hsc.on.ca/HSCMouseLibrary.

The idea for this project was born when a student asked a question and it turned into an entire grade cross multidiscipline collaboration to build a library for the second grade's stuffed mice. After researching and interviewing several experts, the library quickly grew beyond just shelving for books. The grade 2 students built a four-story learning environment for their mice that included working elevators, a café, a mindfulness zone, a rooftop patio, a gender-neutral washroom, a creativity center, a computer lab for research, and even a maintenance room! The students authored and illustrated an abundance of mini books for the book stacks.

Lisa explained that she doesn't really strive to approach facilitating learning with a unit approach. Rather, she considers PBL as more of a mind-set and a process where learning skills and strategies are infused into the project as her class goes along. Barb and Lisa both feel that their students covered far more learning outcomes, skills, and strategies than they ever could have imagined and they're confident the students will remember this experience for many years to come. The confidence, pride, and communication skills alone that the students gained through sharing this project were remarkable.

Their students used conversations, self-reflections, peer assessments, rubrics, and expert critique during their Mouse Library project. (There are samples of all the assessments they used in the blog.) Lisa appreciates that this one project truly changed her approach to education. Facilitating her first PBL project was liberating, and the energy and engagement in her students was remarkable. This project was featured on the local news channel's "Advertising Excellence in Education" segment; it has appeared in blogs and on Twitter and has been the highlight of her students' learning.

Barb and Lisa advise all educators to learn everything they can about PBL and jump right in. Do not worry about having everything planned out in advance. Give yourself some wiggle room and enjoy the learning journey with your students—you will not regret it!

Brandi Leggett

Rosehill Elementary, Instructional Coach
12 years of teaching experience
Geometry Shoe—Applying Geometry to the Real World

Brandi Leggett took a group of K-2 students and transformed how they learned about geometry. Students discovered how geometry is used in the real world. This unit built on smaller projects all leading to their culmination that is actually driving the unit. Students learned about shapes and lines and were able to describe their attributes and compare/contrast. Students learned the shapes through videos and memorized them. They completed worksheets on them and made some with Play-Doh. This one project covered a number of common core geometry standards from K-2: K.G.2, K.G.3, K.G.4, K.G.5, 1.G.1, 1.G.2, 1.G.3, 2.G.1, 2.G.2, 2.G.3.

Students kicked off the unit by going around the school and looking at shapes. They took photos of different shapes and then discussed why they were used the way they were in the school, but also what shape could replace it and how that would change the architecture of the building. Next, students used a geometry stencil to create a picture combining shapes. They wrote about it and make a stop-motion movie of the object they created. Then, students learned about symmetry by making symmetric masks. They had to discuss their designs and what all the attributes were. Students also read about shapes and then created two- and three-dimensional shapes using marshmallows and toothpicks. After this, students looked at different designs to see how shapes are used in the real world. They then drew a geometric city using some requirements and then were able to design them however they would like.

Finally, the students designed shoes using newspaper and tape but also were able to add on materials. It was supposed to be newspaper and tape, but when the media specialist looked at the shoes, she discussed with Brandi how they could be so much better with materials from the Makerspace. Once one group got their shoes created, everyone just became much more creative. Also, students changed their designs many times. Some failed, so they redesigned and made them much better. Students learned how to persevere and how to combine all their ideas as a team. The students got district administrators shoe sizes and then designed the shoes for them. When they were done, students had to describe all the attributes of the shoe and all the geometry used in them. To complete the unit, all the adults came and participated in a geometry fashion show where the students were able to share the geometry concepts, what they learned, and walk down the red carpet.

Brandi's greatest memory is how excited and proud her students were. She recalls that students who struggled in other academic areas gained so much confidence because they shined with their designs. One student who was normally very shy, walked the runway with confidence, completely shocking her parents. Students could not believe that district administrators actually were able to wear their creations. Brandi's students were able to learn much more because things that were not in the grade-level standards may have been in their shoe. The learning was relevant to them. Brandi supplied us with a few links to showcase the famous fashion show that the students were so proud of: https://www.kansascity.com/news/

local/community/joco-913/shawnee-lenexa/article196790759.html. https://www.youtube.com/watch?v=Rs5of1PSDUk.

Brandi's assessment procedure involved asking questions and also having the students describe their learning. She reviewed the grade-level shapes they needed to know and showed images where students had to be able to say what they are and/or compare them and list their attributes. This allowed Brandi to see who may need more practice. A lot of the assessment was ongoing by observing and listening to group work and prompting for information. Students also took a summative test.

One unique piece of advice Brandi conveyed when using PBL was to start backward. Always look at the standards and what you are trying to accomplish first. Identify the learning targets and then think about ways that it can become relevant to students. Start small and don't try to take on too much at once.

Aubrey DiOrio

Kindergarten Teacher, Brier Creek Elementary School, Raleigh, NC
10 years of teaching experience
PBLclouds

Aubrey DiOrio read the book *Hacking Project Based Learning* by Ross Cooper and Erin Murphy. This started her mind spinning about PBL, and she was eager to pick a project to get excited about and begin the journey with her kindergartners. She discovered a great idea for a meteorologist project which fit in great with the weather unit her class was already doing. She did a wonderful job documenting the journey here in her blog and also on Twitter. https://aubreydiorio.com/2017/04/01/pblclouds-the-story/. https://aubreydiorio.com/2017/04/09/pblclouds-the-reflection/.

Aubrey explained that she used individualized lessons, hand-over-hand guidance, videos she chose, and multiple-choice assessments as a foundation for her PBL project. Her students searched for videos with criteria, made observations, predictions, and checked their predictions. The students also created a weather report using a green screen and information they learned from a meteorologist. Aubrey's students were able to apply the standards to their everyday life. They continue to have conversations about their weather predictions. In her opinion, the PBL never really ended. Their final assessments were given through conferencing with each group, by the video they chose to share about clouds, and by their final green-screen weather report.

Aubrey feels that she now has much more inquiry-based ideals involved in her teaching. She doesn't answer questions, *she helps her students find the answers.* She advises teachers to jump in when it comes to PBL. It won't be perfect. You will make mistakes. It will be messy and chaotic. But it will be so worth it!

Lisa Uesugi and Hazel Tagatac

Island Pacific Academy—4th-grade classroom teachers
15 years and 7 years teaching experience, respectively
Book and Bake Sale—Economics Unit

To begin this unit, Lisa and Hazel's students start by discussing what economics is. They go over economic vocabulary and do mini lessons about scarcity, supply and demand, and past and present assembly lines. They do activities on how to budget, instant gratification and opportunity cost, and creating a business based on their interest and passions.

Through student initiative, they then organized a book and bake sale. The students applied for their positions and got placed in teams. Each team took take care of a different aspect and had decision-making power. The Marketing Team met with the school Advancement Team to learn and partner with them to market the event. They also helped with social media as well as logos, merchandising, and all signage. The Leadership Team met with Admin and Advancement to learn how to lead. They also created a market survey for the school and helped organize the event. The Finance Team met and worked with the school account clerks to work out the budget, spreadsheets, and plan out expenses as well as work as cashiers and reported the totals after the event. The Crew took care of organization and worked with facilities. They were our workforce. All students were mindful of their deadlines.

During this time Lisa and Hazel also had guest speakers come in to talk about small businesses. They also got a panel of small business owners to come in to meet with the students. The students were able to ask these business owners questions about why and how they started their business. They were also given the opportunity to ask these business owners advice about their own event. There was a field trip to the Four Seasons where they learned about customer service and marketing. They followed a cookie from concept, marketing, creation, price point, and sale. All culminating in a school-wide sale where they worked every aspect of the event, also becoming customer service reps, created the entertainment (they wrote a jingle), and documented it. It was a huge success, almost selling out and making well over what was projected. This year when they implement, they will have rubrics that are teacher/student created for each team.

Lisa and Hazel noticed that there were a couple of students on the marketing team, specifically, who were able to problem-solve creatively and use their artistic talent to market. They were amazed and completely excited to see that their skills worked and shined in this arena.

Lisa has also been using "discussion sticks" so that the students take charge of the discussions. That activity blows her away every time. These fourth graders discuss respectfully, meaningfully, and intelligently. Lisa maps out the flow of the conversation using the Equity Maps app. The app provides quantified data that she uses to conference with students to help them reflect on how areas for growth in their collaboration skills. She will be trying "fish bowl" next.

Lisa implements multiple reflections and discussions based on their prior and current knowledge and how they are connecting it to the content. Lisa proclaims that she is excited to teach again. The depth of knowledge is incredible, and the kids are constantly amazing her. She knows these are the kinds of projects the kids will remember for a very long time. PBL is a way to get students engaged in real-world problem-solving while incorporating the standards across the curriculum. The students walk away excited, with so many soft and hard skills, as well as a deeper understanding of the world around them. They are also extremely proud of themselves and of their classmates. Talk about a long-term bonding lesson!

Jim Cash

Peel District School Board, Ontario, Canada, Modern Learning Resource Teacher
25 years of teaching experience
Learning Design by Making Games

After an initial period of developing basic competency in Scratch, Jim Cash asked his students to "design a game in Scratch that makes learning fractions fun and easy for younger students." This was a PBL activity that had several dimensions of purpose and intention. In terms of curriculum, it addressed mathematics and language arts outcomes in grades 2, 4, and 5.

Students experienced firsthand the real problems and challenges of design thinking with an authentic product and an authentic audience. Students reflected and created a design-thinking flowchart based on this nine-month PBL activity. Other outcomes related to mathematics and computational thinking were also achieved.

Primarily, informative assessment practices focused on collecting evidence of learning through observations, conversations, interviews, reflections, processes, and recording the development of the products themselves that were being created throughout the activity. More details about assessment issues are contained in this resource Jim created to communicate this project to other teachers: http://bit.ly/LDbMG.

PBL is an effective model of learning that respects students' voice and choice, allows for differentiation, and allows for students to find their own way to the understandings of the content and skills involved in creating the product for that PBL activity.

Amy Valentino

Slackwood Elementary School, Lawrence Township Public Schools
17 years of teaching experience
SOLE

Prior to PBL, Amy Valentino did not use the SOLE (Student-Organized Learning Environment) approach with her second graders, but she had been very eager to learn the approach. Over time, she was able to develop and implement SOLE into her classroom, and she now partners with another second-grade teacher to hold weekly SOLE sessions. They begin by modeling how to utilize appropriate and accurate websites to conduct research. Students practice in pairs researching a topic as well as learning how to take notes. They then learn to research and answer a Big Question (a question that has many possible answers such as "How does erosion occur? How can kids learn without going to school?"). Students learn to utilize Google Classroom and ultimately work together to create presentations using Google Slides or Docs. Students learn to add pictures and videos, change fonts and backgrounds, and add transitions. At the conclusion of each session, the students share their presentations with peers. Teachers act as facilitators and technological troubleshooters. Students learn they must collaborate, communicate, and create with their peers and utilize each other if they experience difficulties with technology or research.

The session begins by the teachers presenting the Big Question in the grade-level-shared Google Classroom. Students self-select work partners and gather materials. They have twenty minutes to research and twenty minutes to create presentations. During this time, students are highly engaged and creative. They are excited and proud to share their presentations. Often, students continue to work on their presentations at home and resubmit them to their teachers. They work together to problem-solve and troubleshoot both research and technical difficulties. During the presentations, Amy and her colleagues assess how well the question was answered, how well the students were able to research and write their data in their own words, and how well they can use the technology available to them.

Amy explained that when the SOLE sessions begin, students often struggle immensely in learning to take notes (and not copy), sign into their Google accounts (brand new to them), and learn how to use Google for Education apps. Amy's colleague that she coteaches weekly SOLE sessions with is always doubtful that it will all come together, but Amy reminds her that patience and trust is vital and with time, the students begin to create amazing things. The teachers are trying to establish and provide real-world learning to help better prepare them for their futures in working technology as well as working relationships. Amy recalls how amazing it feels to sit in the back of the room as an audience member, watch the students navigate her laptop without her, listen to them present their research, and be amazed at how they figured out how to add pictures, change backgrounds, insert videos, add transitions, change themes, and more in Google Slides.

Although SOLE and PBL require more initial preparation by the teacher, the outcome is completely rewarding. Amy has realized that with the proper guidance, modeling, scaffolding, and trust in her students, they can accomplish amazing things while she sits back and observes. They have become the teachers. Being a "risk-taking educator" is something that was new to Amy. Years ago, a new principal at her school encouraged her to try new things in the classroom, and he helped to provide her with new resources to do just that. Somehow, Amy quickly became known for this and is regularly asked to try new ideas, devices, websites, apps, and she's now also asked to help others colleagues use them as well. Now, if Amy likes an idea, she will try it out. If it works, great! If not, she tries something else. Amy has become more fluid and flexible and really embraces a student-led classroom.

Go to THEPBLPLAYBOOK.com for more resources, materials, and guiding questions about this chapter.

CHAPTER 10:

The Homework Problem (and How PBL Solves It)

XOXXOXOOXO

It was toward the end of the third marking period a few years ago when my math teachers in our middle school came up to me.

"AJ, I think we've got a problem, hoping you can help."

"Sure," I said, "what's going on?"

"Well, it's kind of weird. Almost all of our students are turning in their homework. We usually check for completion, but when this started happening it was unusual."

I responded, "That's a good thing, right?"

"Yes, it was good that they were turning in homework. But the odd piece was that it was all correct. All of the steps were right; the solution was right."

I waited to hear more . . .

"And we think they are cheating. We aren't sure how, but something is going on. Even the online homework we are assigning is coming back correct, so it's not like kids are copying each other on the bus like the old days."

"Okay, I can check into it and see what we find."

At that point, I wasn't sure what was going on, but it did seem odd. I know from when I was teaching, and now being an administrator, normally you don't get 100% of the students turning in homework.

A few weeks later, they came back to me.

"It hasn't stopped. And now we are getting complaints from parents."

I laughed, even though they seemed serious.

"Why are you getting complaints?"

"Well," she said, "our kids are getting 100 percent on every piece of homework, and yet, they are not passing the quizzes and tests. Parents are wondering how this is possible, and quite frankly, so are we."

Hmm. I thought for a moment before responding, "Let's ask a student, and see what they say. Can't hurt!"

The next period I headed to the library commons area where some students were working on math during a study hall. I asked one of the students what was going on with math homework, and if she was getting all the answers right.

The student said, "Oh yeah, I think everyone just uses Photomath now. We are allowed to use it, right? It's just like a calculator, right?"

I asked to see it in action.

What happened next caught me by surprise. Not because I couldn't believe it, but because it changed the way I viewed math forever.

She would pick up her iPhone (or maybe it was an Android) and open up an app. Then flicking over to a clear screen, she would hover the phone over a specific problem in her textbook.

It was nothing short of magic. If by chance, someone had been transported here from even twenty years ago they might not have believed it was possible.

The phone immediately (I mean it was quick!) overlaid the problem, multiple steps, and a solution all in a row on her screen. She jotted down the answers on her piece of paper and went on to the next problem.

"That is Photomath?" I questioned.

"Yep. It's a free app."

"Are you allowed to use that? Is it something your teacher uses in class?"

"Um, I don't think Ms. Carter knows about it . . . but no one ever said we couldn't use it. Am I in trouble?"

I told her she wasn't in trouble at all and continued to ask a few more questions about how the app worked. But there wasn't much to learn. It worked just as I saw it work. I quickly Googled the app on my phone and found this video (which is eerily similar to what I saw in the library that day): ***Photomath 2.0 from MicroBLINK on Vimeo*** (https://vimeo.com/147764920?scrlybrkr=42f32365).

We tend to hear stories all the time of computers doing "human things" and impacting productivity, but this time it was different.

And Photomath is not the only app out there that does it. In fact, it may not be the best at this process.

This Verge author wrote about his experience with Socratic (another math-solving app that answers questions from other subjects as well), that seems to take this process to the next level:

> *I pointed it at 2x + 2 = 7x – 5, which I wrote down at random, and it gave me a 10 step process that results in x = 7/5. It has trouble with word problems, but if you can write down a word problem in math notation it shouldn't be an issue. I also tried it on a weird fraction from an AP algebra exam, which it kind of failed at, but then I swiped over and it was showing me this graph, which included the correct answer:*

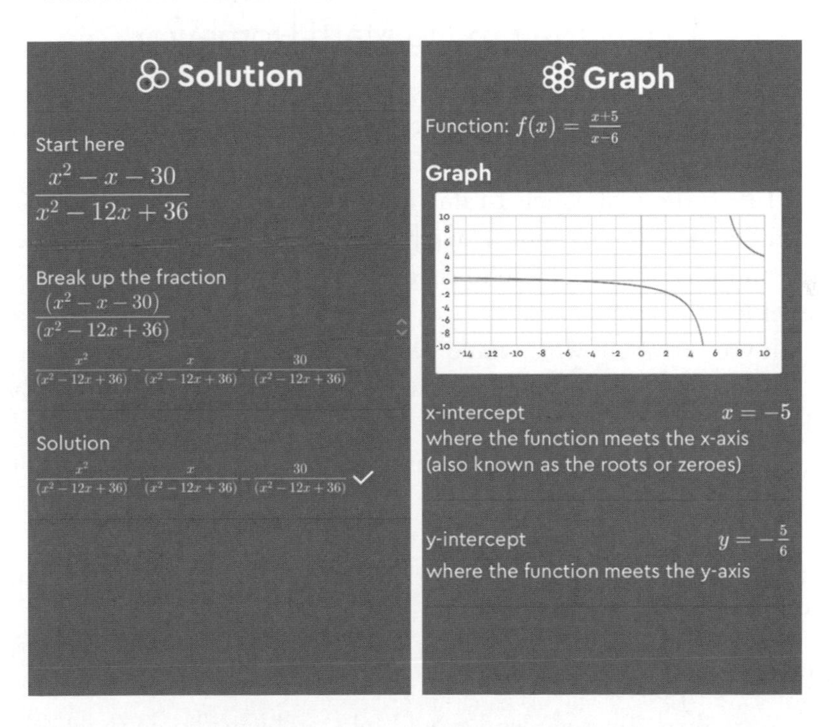

> *I love this app, not just because it would've helped 8th grade Paul out of a jam, but because it's such a computery use of computers. You use the tiny computer in your pocket to be basically smarter than you already are. It's technology that augments a human brain, not just a distraction.*
>
> *The creator of Socratic just open sourced its step-by-step solver, called* mathsteps. *There are a lot of computer-based algebra solvers out there, but for Socratic they had to do some extra engineering to get at the steps a human would need to solve the same problem.*

This is a serious evolution of the calculator. No human input needed to solve equations, only a smartphone, and the app with a camera.

So, I went back to my math teachers, ready to show them the app that would end math homework as they knew it . . . forever.

A New Way to Do Math Homework

I know there is a big debate over the practicality of homework in general. I also know that this is not the first time someone has tackled the idea of doing math homework differently (Flipped Classroom, anyone?).

That being said, when I came back to our math teachers to show them Photomath, they took a long hard look at their instructional practice, and what they could do to change things up in order to give kids a better learning experience.

It was not about what would be easy to do on their end.

It was not about using the latest and greatest technology to combat Photomath.

It was not about taking the focus away from mathematical concepts.

It was about the learning.

The teachers quickly made up their mind. There was no reason to continue giving the same homework each night to students who could answer every question with Photomath.

Were there times they would still give problems and practice them in class? Of course.

Were there times students would take problems home to work on and study? Of course.

Yet, in the long run, something needed to change in order for the students to be successful.

They brainstormed a number of options that included three viable solutions:

1. Give no homework and only optional problems they could solve and work on at night.
2. Flip the classroom (watch instructional videos for homework).
3. Have students create their own video tutorial (screencasts) explaining how they solve problems.

Although options 1 and 2 were still going to be used, our teachers selected the video tutorials as the main focus for homework moving forward in most math classes.

The Nightly Math Project

The Buck Institute describes **Project-Based Learning** as a teaching method in which students gain knowledge and skills by working for an extended period of time to investigate and respond to an authentic, engaging, and complex question, problem, or challenge.

In Buck's model for Gold Standard PBL, the Essential Project Design Elements are:

- ***Key Knowledge, Understanding, and Success Skills****—The project is focused on student learning goals, including standards-based content and skills such as critical thinking/problem-solving, communication, collaboration, and self-management.*
- ***Challenging Problem or Question****—The project is framed by a meaningful problem to solve or a question to answer, at the appropriate level of challenge.*
- ***Sustained Inquiry****—Students engage in a rigorous, extended process of asking questions, finding resources, and applying information.*
- ***Authenticity****—The project features real-world context, tasks* and *tools, quality standards, or impact—or speaks to students' personal concerns, interests, and issues in their lives.*

- ***Student Voice & Choice****—Students make some decisions about the project, including how they work and what they create.*
- ***Reflection****—Students and teachers reflect on learning, the effectiveness of their inquiry and project activities, the quality of student work, obstacles and how to overcome them.*
- ***Critique & Revision****—Students give, receive, and use feedback to improve their process and products.*
- ***Public Product****—Students make their project work public by explaining, displaying and/or presenting it to people beyond the classroom.*

We were already making the shift as a district toward authentic PBL across subject areas, and our teachers believed this was the perfect opportunity to give PBL a shot at tackling the math homework issues.

For each unit, our teachers would now define a math project that would last the entire unit but would be worked on nightly by each student (or group of students depending on the class, subject, and age).

Each project had three phases.

Phase 1

First, students would create their own video tutorials (screencasts) solving math problems that were relevant to the concepts being taught during the unit.

This would include math problems that were teacher provided, problems they found online, and in a textbook or resource.

The screencasts would be created using tools such as Screencast-o-matic or Screencastify, and they would have the students' voice overlay the writing of a problem and solution on a whiteboard.

The teachers would have students share their screencasts with other students during the class and reflect on the steps they took to solve each problem, pointing out teachable moments throughout the video.

Phase 2

The second part of the project involved choice. The student (or group) had to create their own word problem or puzzle that represented the mathematical concepts. The goal was to create a problem that was challenging for others students to solve, and would be one they would have to work through.

In order to do this, the students had to go through a sustained inquiry process in which they tested different problems and ways to display the problem (as a puzzle or word problem). This involved having test groups to answer their problem and developing ways to make sure it was "Photomath" proof.

Phase 3

The last part was all about problem-solving with time constraints. The students had a chance to solve each other's word problems or puzzles and time how long it took them to solve it correctly (if they could). The result would be in one group winning the prize for difficulty and clarity.

By far the most important piece of this last phase is what happened after the challenges were solved and completed. The students would get together in roundtable reflections and talk about what went well, what didn't, and what they learned about this concept throughout the process. The final project created opportunities for more learning and students mastered the skill of not only solving these problems but also creating them.

How Are We Solving Our Problems?

These teachers took a creative approach to solving the problem of the world changing rapidly and their practice being impacted at its very core.

They could have easily tried to continue giving the same type of math homework knowing that programs like Photomath existed.

They could have balked at PBL in math class and focused on a more traditional "I do, We do, You do" approach.

But they worked together to solve a problem with a better way of doing things.

Not an easier way.

A better way.

Project-based learning takes a lot of work to plan and put together on the teacher end. It takes time to tweak and iterate and make better during and after the project is complete. Yet, that is what we are here for.

We are here to provide students with learning opportunities that they could not get somewhere online. We are here to give kids the support and challenge they need to be successful in any type of environment.

When we see challenges, do we treat them like opportunities to do things better, or hope for a solution that can get us back to an old way of doing things?

This approach to the homework problem hasn't only taken place in my school, it has happened at many places around the world including Samantha Cruz's math classroom.

Samantha Cruz

North Broward Prep School
5 years of teaching experience
The Art of Triangles

Samantha Cruz used the driving question: How can you use congruent triangles to create a mosaic work of art? From this, her PBL project was born.

Students completed assignments based on what they were learning in each lesson using exploratory learning. The students write a summary about what they did in each lesson and put it into a report about their work of art. The summary is checked on a formative assignment and then revised for their summative report. Then, they completed part of their mosaic of a picture that they chose using rules that they wrote. Students seem to enjoy the activity although sometimes they get frustrated.

Samantha decided to try PBL because she really wants students to be engaged in what they are learning. They are so used to the teacher showing them how to do math rather than actually understanding how to do it. Samantha teaches them formulas and methods, but they don't truly understand the reasoning behind the method. Because of this, they forget immediately after they are given a test or quiz. This year, Samantha has focused on teaching them how to figure things out and problem-solve. They use different resources to figure out the best way to approach a problem, rather than her teaching them how she would approach everything. Samantha values the learning process and their ability to problem-solve more than the outcome. They are graded on their work, not just their answer. They are also graded on their openness to take risks, not just on whether they got it 100% correct.

Samantha had some students who loved doing this project. One student would take her poster home every day to do more work on it and that really made it turn out amazing! Others struggled to get it done or put little effort into it. They were required to fill up the entire space completely with triangles. Some also had trouble making it look like their original picture. Some of them had trouble connecting the triangles and had a lot of open space between them. One student struggled doing this on the first section, but later on figured out how to do it a better way. Samantha let him know that she was grading him on his ability to revise his work and improve, not just on what they did each day. The fact that he improved his method would help him get a better score.

In the end, Samantha thought the project was successful overall. She has ideas on how to simplify it for next year and get better results. As of now, she has some amazing artwork on her wall that students created using triangles. One of them includes a mosaic of *Starry Night* made completely out of triangles. Others did a logo of their favorite sports team. Some did their favorite animal. They really look amazing!

One thing that Samantha made very clear to the students from day one was that she was learning as much as they were. This was the first time she was diving into PBL. She knew that her methods were not perfect. The students all knew that Samantha was relying on them to help make the method a little better. Each year she includes surveys at the end of each project where students are able to say what worked and what didn't. They let Samantha know what they think should be changed. Overall, the feedback has been very positive with some criticisms.

Samantha's advice includes telling educators not to be afraid to try new things, be transparent with the students if you are trying something new, and encourage the students to take risks as well. Prepare the students from day one by explaining the mind-set you want them to have.

Go to THEPBLPLAYBOOK.com for more resources, materials, and guiding questions about this chapter.

CHAPTER 11:

PBL and the Power of Partnerships

XOXXOXOOXO

Jill Weaver

Valley View Junior High, 8th-grade science teacher
15 years of teaching experience
The Project: How the Rubber Meets the Road

Jill Weaver used PBL to teach her students how to deflect the water from the tread to prevent hydroplaning. They then built, tested, redesigned, and tested again. The best performance designs were sent to Goodyear, and they used their software to evaluate them. They then had a conference with their design team.

Students worked through their understanding of contact forces as they saw how the water interacted with their tread during testing. Jill and her class still did background research and created force diagrams, but in PBL the force diagrams went with their test modeling. Students did a lot of testing and documenting results which resulted in very well-done data tables; each student kept an engineering design log. They went through the engineering and design principles, and there was a lot of redesign and testing to make improvement to tread designs. The designs were evaluated during testing and that is how the best designs were chosen. Jill also did career connections with this unit and looked at what opportunities existed in these fields. Students loved talking to the test drivers that took Ford Mustangs to Nevada to test tires for performance and compared that to our test model. Junior high students are going to be driving cars in the near future so this topic was interesting to them, and they were very competitive due to the best test models being evaluated by Goodyear tire and rubber.

Jill had one gifted learner her first year using PBL that had been closed off to learning, and he has come alive with PBL instruction. His confidence has been restored, and he shines like a superstar when he works through a PBL. Highlight of the year for Jill was watching this team complete building a hydraulic arm to move toxic barrels to a new safe location.

Student retention of the content improved and student self-evaluation showed that the interest level for the topic of study improved. Overall, scores on this content standard in unit testing improved. When Jill did her first PBL, she wanted to make all of her units PBL. Jill's advice is to take your time in the conversion process as it is very time consuming trying to re-create your entire course of study. Jill has since tried to create one new PBL each year.

Beth Wilson

Chattanooga, Tennessee
Red Bank Elementary, 4th-grade teacher
15+ years of teaching experience
Early American Museum

A few years back, Beth Wilson met with her principal to talk about wanting to try to teach in a different way. The principal was interested in listening to Beth but needed more info, so Beth researched and found the BIE site that talked about Project-Based Learning. Beth went down that "rabbit hole" and continued to find ways to make teaching fun for the kids. Beth says that as a fifty-four-year-old teacher, these last few years of teaching have definitely reenergized her. She has a genius time built into her literacy block—every day. Her dream would be to find a way to have all learning happen in PBL, so much that the students don't notice the difference between the subject areas. Beth is a fourth-grade teacher in a self-contained classroom; she tries to introduce students to concepts and learning that will encourage them to be lifelong problem-solvers. Beth also has an intergenerational program called iGen. She takes her students to the local senior living facility where they share their learning with the residents.

For an "invention"-type PBL project, students interviewed the residents of the senior living facility. The task was to find out what their "customers" needs and wants were. After the interviews were completed, students sketched out ideas of items they could invent. Beth grouped students according to similar ideas. They created, tested, and then went back to do a *Shark Tank*-type pitch to the residents. The local TV station came and filmed the presentations. It was a great experience and a wonderful way to learn community involvement.

For her Early American Museum project, students study early America from Columbus to just before the American Revolution. As they study the areas, students make interactive artifacts to add to the museum. The goal is to have the rest of the elementary students come to the museum and learn about early America. Each of the five classrooms is a different time in the early history. This project incorporates all subject areas. The students are allowed to specialize in an area of interest. The students are motivated to learn and research. They enjoy presenting. Confidence and teamwork have improved. Twenty-first-century skills!

Beth can attest to the incredible qualities PBL brings to her students. It has rekindled her passion for teaching, and she has since become a catalyst for her school to go to STEM and PBL in all grades.

Angie Ramey

LaGrange, IL, Advanced Academics ELA Specialist
22 years of teaching experience
United States Refugee Admission Reform

This unit was developed for a small group of eight advanced ELA sixth-grade students. When they were in fifth grade, one thing Angie Ramey learned about them was they had a keen interest in social justice issues and humanitarian causes. Alan Gratz published a book in 2017 called *Refugee* that tells three refugee stories: 1939, Josef who is Jewish; 1994, Isabel of Cuba; and 2015, Mahmoud from Syria. The book was perfect for the CCSS addressing point of view and perspective, as well as opinion writing standards. Angie believed there would be high interest, but also the possibility to explore problem-based learning combined with a blended learning environment. Because Angie is not a classroom teacher and works with these students only three times per week for

20–30 minutes, she worried a blended learning PBL project would not be possible. Angie wrote the unit with the support of Dr. Kathy Schuh, professor at The University of Iowa College of Education. Dr. Schuh pushed Angie to move beyond "I don't have a classroom, so this cannot work." She learned with her encouragement that a PBL *can* work when you're in a specialist role, and to always be open to growth and innovation for kids.

Angie admits it's been a challenge but has turned out simply amazing. This group of students is exploring their complex and messy problem that says, "How should the US decide who enters the country as refugees, how many refugees should the US allow to enter, and how should the US support refugees once they are here?" They are examining current policy since January 20, 2017, past policy, and if there should be any change/reform. The book *Refugee* gives them insight into the lives of refugees, and they are using real-life practice and really thinking about where they stand as individuals and as a group.

Angie is currently using the Schoology Learning Management System (LMS) to organize and engage students during their PBL. This is where they are keeping their group norms, media files, research, dyad folders, discussions, questions, and the like. Using a blended learning approach with a PBL and a small group has been very exciting for Angie. Aside from their research, they are figuring out and writing a request to Skype with Illinois US Senators Tammy Duckworth and Dick Durbin to share their final proposal for US refugee policy. One idea the students have locally, as a result of their research, is looking at how the district provides orientation to new students who do not speak English. Do they have an interpreter who speaks their native language? Can schools set up a like-language buddy for the new student? An increase in positive interdependence, accountable talk, authentic dyad and full group interaction, personal independence, engaged participation and discourse, motivation to create, write, and apply beyond the classroom. All learners benefit from PBL, but Angie felt that this homogeneous group of like-ability middle-schoolers would really thrive in the PBL instructional design. She felt that Schoology and Blended Learning were the key to success. For Angie, watching these students work together, dig deep to try to understand US policy and how they feel, and what they would do has felt like stepping into a mini-State Department.

What Angie would like any PBL educator to remember is that you are not alone. Preferably any PBL plan will be developed in a collaborative environment with a team of enthusiastic teachers, but there are amazing beacon resources accessible to all. There are recipelike books for those who want a linear step-by-step process to follow, to websites with planning, organizational, and assessment tools. There are blogs, discussion groups, and Twitter accounts of support.

"Let us put our minds together
and see what life we will make for our children."
—Sitting Bull

Bonny Skutch

Central Elementary, Wilmette, IL; Differentiation Support Teacher
15 years of teaching experience
Follow the Feet to the Alice Moseley Museum

Bonny Skutch invited Gerilyn Bleau, a museum curator, to speak to her class about what it takes to run a museum and teach them about Alice Moseley, the local folk artist featured in the museum. They asked her about challenges that she faces and if they could help with that. She mentioned that they had many people come from out of town to the museum, but not many locals visit the museum. Bonny's students took on this problem and used the Creative Problem Solving process to help brainstorm, and select and implement solutions to help get more local visitors into the museum. The students realized there was a frequently visited duck pond just steps from the museum. They decided to paint duck feet on the sidewalk leading from the pond to the museum with a sign saying "Follow the Feet to the Alice Moseley Museum." Students presented their proposal at a city council meeting and found sponsors to fund the project. Gerilyn stayed in close contact with the class the entire time they were working on their project and gave them her feedback. She came and visited the class a couple of times to consult with them, ask questions, and answer their questions. She was an invaluable partner throughout the whole process, and she truly believed in the ability of these fifth-grade kids to change their world.

Students were broken into task forces that focused on one element of the problem and became investigators, makers, writers, and experts on their element. Bonny is proud of the fact that her students have been empowered. They discovered a problem and found a solution and implemented that solution. They spoke with real professionals about their problems and work. They learned all the content they were supposed to learn, but they learned people skills, problem-solving skills, and *real*-life skills as well.

One of the most heartwarming feelings that can come from these projects is the tremendous support of community, as we've seen mentioned many times in the book. This project was no exception. Bonny also had tremendous help and support from her community. She had a friend who was very involved in the community who donated the paint. Another friend with a jigsaw cut out a sample of three sizes of duck-feet stencils for the class to take to the student council meeting, one of the City Councilmen made up T-shirts to commemorate the painting day and bought lunch for the class at a local restaurant as a surprise for Bonny and her students. So many of the parents of her students showed up on painting day to help them paint.

Bonny shares an amazing memory regarding a student (let's call him Jeremy) who was kind of a tough guy, class clown, and didn't care much about school. Mind you, this was a gifted class, so he had shown that he was very intelligent, but he didn't have much motivation to do well in school. He was in foster care at the time and hadn't had an easy life. Bonny let her students choose which task force they wanted to be on (paint, signage, city council research, or speakers). Jeremy chose to be a speaker. Bonny was a little nervous about his decision because of his lack of motivation outside of this project. Jeremy shined. It was amazing to watch. He wrote part of the speech with the others on his task force, presented it on his own to other students in the class to seek their feedback, rewrote his speech, tweaked it, practiced it, and perfected it. The night of the City Council meeting he brought note cards with him (Bonny had no idea he was going to do that) and delivered his part of the speech flawlessly and confidently. As a teacher, the look on his face after his speech and after the city council unanimously approved the proposal was one of the most rewarding gifts Bonny has ever been given.

Jeremy was so proud. His classmates and the parents in attendance complimented him on his demeanor and speech and asked if he was going to go into politics. Bonny was proud of him, and proud that she and his classmates had found a way for him to feel empowered and to imagine a narrative for his future that he had probably never imagined before.

While there were so many wins with this project, Bonny is sure there were struggles too, like trying to find a good company to make their sign, and almost running out of time on painting day, but they seem overshadowed by all the wins. Her students were connected to their local government and learned how to make their voices known in their town and that their voices matter. Bonny's group of about fifteen kids worked cohesively as a team to accomplish a large goal and supported each other through it. Their little class was connected with members of the community and their learning environment extended miles beyond the four walls of the classroom.

Bonny knows that PBL has led her to see the skills she has to teach as possibilities for real-world interaction and problem-solving. It has torn down the walls of her classroom and busted through her own limited knowledge to pull in a community of experts who can collectively take her students farther than she could from the front of her classroom.

Charles J. Laurent

Rocky Hill School, 4th-grade teacher
20+ years of teaching experience
Caretakers of History

For this historical-minded PBL project led by Charles Laurent, students partnered with a local historic house museum to raise community awareness of the museum and to make it more child-friendly. Charles displayed outstanding documentation of the project, and a good understanding of it can be found here: http://bit.ly/2zddG3w. The time line included on the website showcased the project process in which the students created and presented to a group of adults and administrators. This was an immersive and authentic experience during which learners used their knowledge of colonial history to make a difference within their larger community. Charles explains that the learners were engaged and motivated to learn history because they understood that the content was crucial to developing ideas to their partner museum. Charles utilized rubrics, presentations, and reflection journals to serve as assessments.

PBL has reinvigorated the way Charles's students acquire knowledge and understanding. Sustained inquiry paired with an authentic driving question, deliverables, reflection, and collaboration have contextualized learning for them in ways he could never have imagined. They know the "why" of what they are learning and are invested 100%.

Charles advises that finding others to help is a helpful tool in taking on PBL; give the kids a voice and choice, plan . . . plan . . . plan, spend time developing a genuine driving question, be prepared for the project to go in a different direction than you had hoped, enjoy the process, and have fun!

Kristin Hundt and Katie Bielecki

Holt, Michigan—6th-grade educators
10 years of teaching experience
Building Equity, Building Outdoor Spaces

Kristin Hundt and Katie Bielecki design their integrated language arts and social studies curriculum around developing empowered global citizens who understand how to utilize their voices through choice. This teaching pair did not intentionally initiate PBL with their learners. It came to fruition by giving (their) students voice and choice during their first year of collaboration with each other, and it facilitated this wonderful change in their teaching and in their school which they have continued ever since. This PBL exploration was also the catalyst to the implementation of Genius Hour in their classroom.

Kristin and Katie study all sorts of global issues with their students while also continuing to look at their own community. Their students were shown video footage of the school's outdoor spaces (playing four square by the dumpsters, a large field that used to be a parking lot) and some footage of a school in the district down the road, serving the same population of children, that had basketball hoops, playground equipment, swings, and outside places to eat and gather. The students were stunned and rightfully frustrated at the inequity of resources and felt the same injustice as they had in other global units of study on topics like food, water, and immigration. They wanted to act! So Kristin and

Katie facilitated that, integrating all subjects and technology as they researched, surveyed, collected, and analyzed data, drew up-to-scale maps with plans, wrote grants and letters to stakeholders, and ultimately began to build outdoor spaces at their school where there were none before. The authenticity of this PBL lies in the fact that the students saw the problem and wanted to act.

This teacher team invited a contractor who'd been in their building giving some estimates on other projects to come check out their space after school. They shared with him that their kids had all sorts of visions and ideas for spaces in and around Hope School. They invited him to come and speak with the students about their ideas. He spoke with his boss, the owner of Hayhoe Construction in Holt, Michigan. The owner returned to their classroom for a community meeting (which happens daily in their classroom as an opportunity to share ideas, connect, and greet each other, hence building community, each day). She arrived to see their dreamings and drawings of the outdoor space turned outdoor classroom which was their dream. Once the community meeting discussion commenced, she could see the students were quite serious about enhancing their space and impacting their school community by doing so. The owner called Kristin and Katie at the close of the day to share with them that she'd been so inspired by the students' ideas and vision that she wanted to match a grant that the students had already secured through the Education Foundation in Holt. She also wanted to donate labor and materials to make the project happen. Within four weeks a new outdoor space was situated!

Over the years, as they've continued this project over the course of several years, this project has continued to evolve with each new group of students that enters their team able to make their own adjustments and enhancements. They have built an outdoor classroom directly from student ideas and vision, made a garden, and purchased a GaGa Ball Pit for outdoor playground equipment. Their mission to foster voice and choice with this PBL continues today.

Kristin and Katie align the ideas that students are dreaming up with the sixth-grade learning targets over time collecting maps, argumentative pieces of writing, group work, assessing comprehension of reading, data and analysis of data, scientific observations, and surveys of the land,

and are able to have all of that count toward sixth-grade standards in all subjects. The sixth-grade standards that this specific PBL activity have experience covered lent itself to include informational reading standards, argumentative writing, speaking/listening, math geometry standards, science ecosystem studies standards, and social studies studying of global issues and topics.

As you can imagine, one of their struggles was opening Pandora's Box as one idea led to another . . . simply the magnitude of what they wanted to have happen and that they wanted it all to happen yesterday! Once the kids were turned on to the injustice in the community and they were able to get their ideas on paper, submit ideas to the learning community and eventually to the business collaborators, the work really came to life and moved.

In summary, Kristin and Katie feel that they now have complete student engagement; Kristin and Katie are passionate learners who recognize the impact of giving students voice and choice in their everyday lives. This voice and choice motivates learning—they are motivated with emotion inspired by the impact that *students* have had on *their* community and with the outcome of real change for their school. Having the learning be integrated is a wonderful way for students to have multiple entry points and be able to show mastery of multiple topics. They want to do this work. Each group of students gets to leave their own unique mark on their outdoor spaces each year. Consequently, every year looks a little different. Doing this particular PBL opportunity shows them what students can accomplish, change, and build while learning. It reaffirmed how important it is to give voice and choice—to really listen to your students and their interests and bring those into the classroom. It also began the implementation of Genius Hour in their team so their students could examine passion and interests on an individual level.

Go to THEPBLPLAYBOOK.com for more resources, materials, and guiding questions about this chapter.

CHAPTER 12:

PBL in the Community (Local and Real)

XOXXOXOOXO

Erin Loch

Upper Dublin High School, 10th-grade environmental science teacher

11 years of teaching experience

Thirteen overlooked students challenged to solve problems by their local zoo: "The Golden 13"

Since attending training at the 2009 Real World Navy Challenge on project-based learning (PBL), Erin Loch has been certain to implement several whole-class projects in her environmental science courses each year. Projects have ranged from proposing a restoration plan for a local pond to creating a Wikipedia page, but the most rewarding always include community involvement. With PBL, the teacher is commonly *not* the expert. Therefore, it's important for students to get into the community to learn from and collaborate with the real experts. Erin's favorite projects involve students connecting with professionals in the community and developing the project around the input of multiple stakeholders. The students learn a great deal more in this manner, and so does she.

One such project, accomplished in a tenth-grade environmental science class, utilized the Philadelphia Zoo's *Unless Contest* as a platform for having students select one environmental issue that they could help resolve. The students chose to think globally and act locally by addressing water pollution in Upper Dublin Township, PA. The local source of their drinking water, the Loch Alsh Reservoir (no relation), is located less than ninety feet from a major highway, PA Route 309. Therefore, students planned to build and plant a buffer zone as well as introduce water-bottle-filling stations to minimize the high school's water footprint and reduce the amount of single-use bottles in landfills, thus improving groundwater quality.

Erin was always interested in attempting a yearlong PBL, and this project presented the ideal opportunity. Best of all, a class from the remedial track quickly proved themselves most worthy of tackling this endeavor. They showed early problem-solving skills, willingness to work together, and excitement for trying something new. Erin decided to take advantage of the small class size and prove to both the administration and the students that this challenge would be more rigorous and educational than a traditional classroom experience. PBL can be done with any and all students.

The students pitched ideas, conducted interviews, created their own team of professionals, leveraged social media to help raise funds for their projects, and created informational videos about their mission for school administrators. They learned time management, task delegation, and how to work with difficult personalities. Erin learned that it was important to step back and, at times, let them fail. Most commonly, "failure" entailed them not meeting their own expectations.

Using the library Makerspace and help from the school librarian, her team employed three-dimensional design to create props for the presentation and stencils for their shirts. Buttons were made to advertise their purpose. Breakout EDU was used along the way for team building and at the final presentation to the zoo for purposes of making their pitch interactive. The director of technology for the district was essential in helping them to meet twenty-first-century skills, employ video technology, and leverage Google tools.

The community was instrumental in helping students get their products finished and publicized. Throughout the project, the class worked with the local township, a sustainable landscape architect, a native plant nursery who donated all the plants, a project supply company, Temple

University students, the athletic department at Upper Dublin High School (UDHS), and the district facilities department. These partnerships required the students to write professional e-mails, ask for donations and permissions, and generally become comfortable speaking to adults in authority.

The students ultimately took second place in the contest. Their greatest moment was the final presentation to the zoo. The students were so dynamic and knowledgeable that the committee—who had preselected the winner before any presentations—changed the format of judging for future contests because the students "wowed" them in person. Still bittersweet for the students, that announcement made second place a perfect win for their teacher. The "Golden 13" exceeded the fundraising necessary to their $2,000 budget and was able to donate the additional funds to Water.org, a charity that provides sustainable water solutions around the world.

Members of the Golden 13 continue to visit the reservoir and check on the status of their buffer zone. Erin has overheard members tell peers with pride that they were responsible for the water bottle fillers. When UDHS students are asked what makes their school "green," many cite the water-filling stations as their first example.

Implementing PBL gave Erin's students greater understanding through *application* of the content knowledge. Breadth of environmental knowledge may be slightly diminished, but understanding goes deeper and is more long-lasting. Additionally, students show measurable growth in needed life skills of collaboration, communication, critical thinking, and creativity. Erin believes so strongly in the benefits of project-based learning that she has developed a yearlong environmental course at UDHS taught entirely in PBL format.

Erin believes that in order for PBL to be truly successful, the teacher needs to act more like a coach than a conventional teacher. Coaches provide encouragement and critique from the sidelines, help participants review "plays," pick them up from failures, and celebrate their successes. Erin warns that one of the hardest things to manage as a teacher new to PBL is not immediately jumping in when students are struggling. You can't play the game for them. Providing guidance without taking the reins is important in allowing them to maintain ownership—

an essential component to success of any PBL. When you feel like they're losing, it's time to take a step back, let them struggle, and find their own way forward. Setbacks are a normal part of life, not losses: and sometimes, second place changes the world—and the future—for the better.

*This photo was published in the *Ambler Gazette*.

Josh Nichols

Stockbridge Community Schools
MI STEM teacher and maker teacher
20+ years teaching experience

Josh Nichols admits he has been teaching in a PBL environment for most of his career, even though he started with direct instruction. Josh's Salmon Release project tells the tale of a class determined to hone their skills to facilitate the continued population of salmon in their area. First, his students created a remotely operated vehicle (ROV) business to promote ROV education in their area. They wanted to demonstrate why ROVs are used in "real-life" situations. They joined the "Salmon in the Classroom" program sponsored by the Michigan Department of Natural Resources (DNR) and decided to use their ROVs to release the salmon they would raise. In November 2012, the school received 222 salmon from the DNR. Unfortunately, all but one died. The students named the survivor, Salmon 222. They also did extensive research to try and figure out why most of the salmon died. They sent their report to the DNR, who decided to give the school a new batch of salmon. While waiting for their new salmon to arrive, the students continued their quest to design and build an ROV that would release the salmon in the spring. The students also educated other students and members of their community about ROVs by making presentations at their local Lowe's store and handling out informational pamphlets.

Josh's class also had the amazing opportunity to send one of their early ROVs to the Pacific island country of Palau with the high school ROV team, to help with a World War II MIA search mission. This was another "real-life" opportunity to use their ROV as a tool. Their primitive ROV actually found a sunken Japanese cargo ship. After this, the students then utilized the skills they had mastered along the way in their previous projects and built the ROV they had been waiting for—the one that would release their salmon. The students partnered with the high school ROV team and built two ROVs equipped with GoPro cameras that captured the salmon being released in a mid-Michigan River. All the salmon were successfully released, including Salmon 222.

After implementing STEM/PBL projects, Josh says the students' state tests scores shot through the roof. Here is an article by Michigan Public Radio entitled "What Grit Can Do for Test Scores." http://stateofopportunity.michiganradio.org/post/what-grit-can-do-test-scores-michigan-classroom-experiment.

Josh recalls that a student named Walker had an almost life-changing experience after his PBL project. Walker had always been interested in copy machines and was curious about how the repairman fixed the school's machines. Once introduced to the copy repairman, he studied their every move. Before too long, Walker started fixing all the machines in the school. Josh and Walker's peers saw a light kick on, and Walker became one of the lead ROV designers. Before long, he even learned how to use a multimeter (keep in mind this was a third grader who never passed a standardized state test) and tested everyone's solder joints, to test continuity. He later started his own computer class in school where he taught fellow students how to take apart computers and upgrade them.

Josh's incredible success did not come without struggles. Finding a way to manage projects that included leadership roles, reflection, fluency, assessments, collaboration, and voice was not an easy task. Over the years, Josh developed a process with incredible results. This is how CrossBraining came about. He knew that every teacher he talked to loved the idea of incorporating engaging, meaningful projects into their classroom, but most didn't do it because it was hard to maintain control without a process. Josh created the CrossBraining App that is both an integrative teacher classroom management system and a student learning system that guides students through four phases of any lesson or project. Students plan, perform, polish, and produce a 45-second narrated video using learning goals from the standards to show content mastery.

As many educators have mentioned, Josh agrees that having a network of PBL supporters around you makes a big difference. Josh had incredible support from his administrator Jim Kelly who gave him the freedom to fail and encouraged him to explore engaging ways to reach his students' individual needs. Josh also had the support of his wife, Angie, who teaches at the same school and helped him rethink the way he managed his PBL lessons. Angie, along with Travis Sparks, who was another lead teacher in this project, used their organization skills to help everyone stay focused on organizing all the moving parts. Travis, Jim, and Angie created a culture where they knew they were going to fail and fail often, but together, they made a system to keep track of those failures and a mind-set to overcome and fix them. They did a lot of things, off the cuff, but the support network they created kept them safe as they developed their system and processes. Josh now continually tells people, "If someone asked me to go back and teach the other way, I would have to quit. PBL has changed my life because it is the way that I wanted to teach. I can see how it has changed the lives of my students."

Two years ago, Josh was asked to sit on the Governor's MiSTEM Advisory Board; now PBL is part of legislation—for any teacher who wants a STEM grant, it must be PBL driven.

Maria Claudia Gimma

Seven Valleys New Tech Academy—Spanish and Media Arts
20 years of teaching experience
City Family, Country Family

In Maria Claudia Gimma's Spanish class, students review family activities, vocabulary, and conjugations as they learn new verb sentences to illustrate the cultural traits of a Latin American country. They use their findings to write a bilingual children's book that will be read to area elementary schools.

Students first watch a cartoon that is about a city mouse and a country mouse to see how this is portrayed to explain the cultural differences found between city and country families in the United States. A driving question is given to the class to start the discussion of how they will complete their own book portraying the different characteristics they will research in a Spanish-speaking country that each student will choose. Once the students figure out the things they may already know about the subject, Maria will help them find information on what they still need to do and will provide small lectures and ideas as she sees needed.

As students work on their project, Maria will allow them the opportunity to seek input from their classmates in order to edit their work. Once the project is completed, students will have the opportunity to present their work to Cornell Latin American Studies students to assure reverence and authenticity. The University students' input will be very valuable for the class in order to finalize their book before reading it to their audience. Students are assessed on their ability to work independently and in a group. Maria provides grammatical and congregational drills throughout, gives them vocabulary quizzes, and provides them with Spanish-written and -speaking opportunities.

Maria has found that by asking questions, doing their own research, and rehearsing their learning to each other in class, the students are able to learn the material in their own way, resulting in retaining the knowledge longer.

Maria can honestly say that she enjoys her role as a language coach and facilitator much more due to the engagement and ownership she sees in her students now. In a way, she learns a lot from them as well as they do their research, or as they themselves come up with different class activities that promote their own learning. PBL is a lot of work; sometimes it can make Maria feel overwhelmed, but as one starts finding a routine that works, the planning is easier, and the more enjoyable the work becomes. Allowing your students to have a choice in the way they learn is a powerful way of teaching.

Kelli Cochran

6th-grade science and pre-AP science teacher
17 years of teaching experience
Solar Ovens for Uganda

For this project, Kelli Cochran and her students learned about thermal energy and types of heat transfer, and as their LAUNCH, they designed and built solar ovens for the people of Uganda.

Kelli taught her students how thermal energy and kinetic energy of particles work and how they behave in different types of heat transfer: conduction, convection, and radiation. They learned about human impact in the PBL prior to this one where they planned, designed, and built a model green home where all rooms and building materials were eco-friendly and built to scale. As their LAUNCH, they displayed these buildings at PT Conferences.

Kelli then showed them three inspirational videos about the people of Uganda, Africa, and their current situation with the dangerous use of smoking huts to cook their food. Three million women and children are dying of the exposure to harmful smoke. Because of the abundance of sunlight in Africa, a healthier alternative to cooking is building solar ovens out of inexpensive materials. After brainstorming about the videos, Kelli asked her students to design two prototypes of solar ovens with consideration of angle of sunlight, reflection and absorption qualities, and durability. They also had a guest speaker, an administrator from the school, who visits Uganda every year through the ministries of his church. He talked about the Ugandan people in depth and the hardships that they face, and he explained the need of solar ovens in the villages that he visits. He surprised the class by saying that he would bring three suitcases full of solar ovens back to his people. Kelli's students now had constraints: a time limit because they were going to Uganda in three weeks, size because they had to fit a lot of solar ovens into the suitcases, weight because it could not go over fifty pounds so he wouldn't have to pay the luggage check-in fee, durability because it had to withstand the African terrain and weather, and effectiveness because it had to absorb and reflect at the right places. Her students were ecstatic and on a mission.

They took the time to write about the pros and cons of solar ovens in an essay format and a sequential writing piece about how to build solar ovens to improve literacy skills. They measured dimensions, weighed their solar ovens, and used protractors to get the angles just right to improve their mathematical skills. They also worked afternoons and weekends at school to make the deadline. They wanted to explain how to reassemble their solar ovens after the trip there because a lot of them had to fold inward to be more compact. They discovered a way to do this: they took a series of pictures and translated their instructions into Swahili and Ugandan based on the area of Uganda he was visiting. The students sent these inside each of the solar ovens. When Mr. Rainwater got to Uganda during fall break, he would send pictures of the Ugandan people using the solar ovens through Facebook. It was an amazing feeling to see actual people using their solar ovens. Kelli's students were extremely empowered during this project. Kelli knew how invested they were in this project when she saw them coming in on Saturdays and staying after school to work. She was very impressed by their dedication.

As for assessments, Kelli graded the two writings that her students did during the unit, their planning guide of research and brainstorming, their two prototype designs and choice of one, testing of the solar ovens by using solar lamps and placing them in front of her classroom window, and the final product.

When Kelli was first starting out, she knew she had to fully try PBL and Design Thinking in her classroom with all of her students to show that it could work. She took the course on Leadership and Innovation, John Spencer's Mastermind Course on Design Thinking, and April Smith's Implementing PBL course. They all taught her how to do PBL and Design Thinking in her classes. Kelli started looking at my NGSS frameworks and seeing which ones went together naturally and how she could work in frameworks from other disciplines. She had always done PBL partially throughout the year but needed to go "all in" and full force. Kelli knew she needed to reinvent the way that she taught to prove that if it worked with all her students, then it could work with all students in a school of innovation.

She eventually met with her superintendent and the rest is history. Kelli didn't realize the amazing things that would happen to her through empowering students. She didn't know that it would lead to her students impacting the world, building confidence in their own learning, help her start a new school in the district, and help Kelli to leave the classroom to become an innovation coach. Kelli admits that she loves the classroom but feels a greater pull to help create systematic change. Kelli feels that everything has lead up to this major event in her life, and God is calling her to make a change.

Andrea Schmuttermair

Colorado STEM Academy, Westminster, CO, primary math and science teacher
13 years of teaching experience
Marine Mission

In Marine Mission, students are working to address the question: Should people inland care about the ocean, and if so, why? In the landlocked state of Colorado, students often have the misconception that their actions do not affect our world's oceans. Once students have discovered that their actions do indeed affect our world's oceans, they will take a deeper look into some of the biggest issues our ocean is facing today. The final goal of this PBL is to create community awareness about these issues, and some students may take this further to come up with ways they (and the community) can help. The final presentations will take place in a community event at the local aquarium in Denver, CO, where students, their families, and the local community will be invited to attend.

Prior to this unit, Andrea Schmuttermair used to teach standards in isolation. They were not a cohesive unit, nor did they connect to real-world issues. Science was taught during science time, math, during math, and so on. The cross-curricular connections were lacking. By creating this PBL unit, Andrea has been able to weave in this theme across all subject areas. Students are reading nonfiction text and learning about text features as they learn about concepts such as overfishing. They're learning to synthesize the information they read and write for a real-world audience to inform them about ocean issues. They are graphing real data from NOAA during math, and collaborating with guest scientists both locally and nationally to learn more about their area of interest. Everything Andrea's students work on during this unit is through the lens of their driving question: Should people inland care about the ocean, and why?

Once students have discovered that their actions do indeed affect the ocean, Andrea and her students look at some of the major issues the ocean is facing. Students have the opportunity to voice which issues they believe are the most important, while being introduced to some they might not initially think of. With Andrea's help, her class came up with categories of various ocean issues the world is facing: overfishing, sustainability, plastic pollution, and climate change. Students were excited as they got to choose what area they wanted to work on. As students learn about their issue in order to create community awareness, she also brings in experts to talk to the students. Andrea has had several scientists either come into the class or Skype with the students to answer questions and give students a real-world picture of these topics. Being able to connect with scientists and outside experts is key for the students in helping them to understand the reality of their research.

Engagement and deeper learning have been the most obvious outcomes, as students have taken ownership of their learning because they have had choice in the direction of their project and there is a purpose for their learning. Passion and drive for learning beyond what is required are the other outcomes Andrea has seen in her students. Students were most excited in creating their presentations and deciding what they would hand out to the visitors to help create awareness about their topic; this ranged from creating bookmarks with a local printing company, to handmade bracelets, and even T-shirts. Students were thrilled when all of their "giveaways" were gone at the end of the night.

Content is assessed throughout the PBL unit rather than at the end. With check-ins (quizzes, writing assignments, both formal and informal assessments) throughout the unit, Andrea can adjust instruction as necessary to clear any misconceptions before the final presentations. Her goal as the teacher is to know exactly where her students are before their final presentation, so that on presentation day, she can concentrate on supporting the students as they present to audiences and evaluate the twenty-first-century skills (i.e., presentation, creativity, etc.). On the final presentation, Andrea likes to get feedback from outside community members; this can include scientists who have been (and even those who haven't been) involved in the project, parents, and other teachers. This feedback helps to give Andrea's final evaluation of the students' learning for this project.

The most memorable outcome was with one particular student. Prior to this project, all this student was interested in was gaming, computer, and programming. Andrea had a hard time getting him excited about things that did not involve these topics. He had difficulty seeing beyond those interests of his. When introduced to this PBL unit, and given the opportunity to build an underwater ROV during the unit, a fire lit inside him. He saw that he could have other interests in addition to gaming, and that his interests could be combined with gaming and programming. He became an ocean ambassador at one of the local ocean organizations that had worked with the class in this project, and, two years later, is still involved in the club. Andrea swears that if she can continue to ignite this kind of passion in her students through PBL, then this is the way to teach.

Not only has PBL engaged her students, it has also engaged Andrea as an educator. She has noticed that she is much more excited about teaching when they have a project going, because she sees how excited her students get. Andrea enjoys finding resources to help them, and connecting with content experts as they help teach her the content so she can better explain it to her students. It has led her to explore community connections, and to seek out professional opportunities to bring different PBL opportunities to her students. One request: Is there room here to add anything in what I wrote about collaborating with others in this paragraph? I'd like to be able to recognize the others who collaborated on this PBL and highlight that here, as the collaboration was crucial to the project's success.

Andrea's words ring true to her experiences in the Marine Mission PBL. Put in the time. Be patient. Do not get discouraged. Collaborate with not only your colleagues, but also with people from various fields of work. And revise, revise, revise. Your project will not be perfect the first time, so take the time to reflect, revise, and go at it again.

Frances Granger

Pike Road Elementary School; Lead Learner
7 years of teaching experience
Community One—Save the Frogs!

Frances Granger's immense understanding of PBL began by reading the book *Just Ask the Children* by Dot Schuler. The following link to the Adobe Spark flyer explains in great detail the project she completed with her students. https://spark.adobe.com/page/mJWMK1PG8Wu8H/.

Frances will tell anyone that she was not the lead contributor to this project. She was simply along for the ride as the students asked questions and decided where they wanted this project to take them. At the time, the school Frances taught at was only a year old. The students were noticing an abundance of frogs on their playground. The children became increasingly worried about the frogs' safety and wondered why there were so many on their playground. Through research, they came to the conclusion that the frogs were there because they had cut down their habitat to build the school. Frances facilitated a wonderful Google hangout with a representative from the Save the Frogs Organization that helped the kids plan their own Save the Frogs Day for their school.

Once Frances saw that this was where she and her class wanted to go, she used the Essential Project Design to help her make sure this project was aligned to the GOLD Standard PBL. She then used The Project Approach website to help organize the actual steps they were going to take. Frances really appreciated their planning charts. It allowed her to not only see the whole project but also break it down into beginning, middle, and end. Many standards were covered in this project. The standards were mostly science based, but they also wrote letters in ELA to ask for permission to have a Save the Frogs Day at school. This activity involved learning about the organization of a letter, grammar, sentences, punctuation, and the like. The students also counted the money raised in math class and answered story problems regarding the frogs on the playground.

Frances recalls one learner who really took the project and ran with it. A boy named Davis set up his own fundraiser outside of school by selling lemonade. To this day whenever Frances sees Davis he is often educating others about how to treat frogs and their importance in the world. Her class raised over $120 that year, which to a group of first graders is a truly amazing contribution to the world.

What Frances had thought in the past were great PBL opportunities, failed in comparison to the famous Save the Frogs project. She admits that at her school she works alongside many incredibly talented educators who are all passionate about the benefits of Project-Based Learning. They share stories of success and failure and encourage one another. Frances stresses that she is very grateful to work in a school system that knows and understands the WHY of Project-Based Learning so that educators can work together through professional learning to determine the HOW.

Julie Luoma, Kristin Schneider, Nathan Wendlowsky, Melissa Pennington

Woodglen Elementary—Adams 12, Five Star Schools (Fourth Grade Team)
Julie Luoma—12 years of teaching experience
Kristin Schneider—2 years of teaching experience
Nathan Wendlowsky—12 years of teaching experience
Melissa Pennington—5 years of teaching experience

Childhood Obesity

This team began their unit with the overarching problem of childhood obesity. According to the Colorado Department of Health, "Colorado has ranked near the top in the nation for leanest adults. However, over 1 in 4 children in Colorado are obese." The students were tasked to come up with a strategy to help decrease childhood obesity so they and their peers could live healthier lives. Standards met through this project included the following: Next Generation Science Standard (fourth grade): CCC.2 and CCC.6 Common Core ELA (fourth grade): W.4.1, W.4.7, W.4.8, W.4.9 RI.4.1, RI.4.9.

This teaching team was looking for a way to increase students' love of learning and make education fun and meaningful again. By having students work on a real-world problem, there was an investment in their learning. Students began doing work at home (on their own without an assignment) and bringing it back to share with their group. This particular PBL project led to district-wide improvements to the schools' lunch menus. One group of students even wrote a grant proposal to purchase a tower garden in order to grow the vegetables they wanted in their school. They wrote the proposal themselves, with guidance from their teacher, and secured the grant. The students continue to maintain the tower, and the plants are producing. This group was in addition to another group who received a $500 award from our school district superintendent to apply to their plans to fight obesity. This was an eye-opening experience for the students *and* the teachers; their students could make a real difference in the community. This success has led to more PBL units and a parent community who appreciates the opportunities their children are being given in school.

For this unit, students are grouped according to their solutions and are responsible for researching (on preselected sites) their solutions through three lenses. As teachers, the team serves as facilitators during this process. Tasks are chunked into manageable pieces. Solutions culminate in a presentation to a panel of experts in which the students propose and defend their solutions. The panelist feedback form the team created was very organized and helpful for assessment purposes. You can check it out here; it may be able to help you relate your own PBL projects to your intended assessments. https://docs.google.com/document/d/1zctBPVnNKpo5o-GZ_cSqLyo4rXqtSpb7U6zFo4J5OhI/edit?usp=sharing.

By the end of the project, the team discovered that students' retention of content knowledge increased dramatically. Students' overall ability to speak and debate knowledgeably on a topic improved a noticeable amount based on parent feedback and teacher observation. There was also an overall higher level of confidence among the students following the PBL experience.

One specific thing that the team agrees helped their PBL to be successful was having the resource of their Digital Literacy Instructor (Nathan Wendlowsky) available to create their Weebly (https://childhoodobesitypbl.weebly.com/) and schedule their panelists and speakers. They also reached out to experts in their fields to come into the classrooms and present. On these days, the teaching team had the students dress up as young professionals. As you might imagine, this added a great level of excitement and ownership of the importance of what they were doing.

This teaching group's testimonial was unique in that there were four main teachers invested in this project and the procedures. They believed passionately about the work they witnessed their students doing, and it was exciting for them to discuss the progress together as educators. They like to remind other PBL newbies not to expect the process to be perfect the first time. Don't be afraid to "go there" with the kids and let them lead the learning through inquiry. Let student questions guide your teaching. It is okay not to be an expert prior to starting a PBL (you will learn along the way). Don't start too big, and as this group learned, a team is greatly helpful.

Jacob Shaw

Plains Junior School; Teacher
17 years of teaching experience
School Constitution

Jacob Shaw's views on students taking notes from a PowerPoint? BORING! Jacob's PBL journey began at the beginning of the 2017 school year. He first heard the term used in a leadership meeting during his preplanning. He was told it was an initiative that his district was trying to push for the teachers. Jacob's initial thought was "Great, another acronym that we have to try to incorporate into the thousands of others we already have with the negative three hours of free time we get."

Fast-forward to October of that school year. Jacob was invited to attend a professional development session the district was holding about PBL. He had started doing a little more research into what PBL truly looked like. He had changed the environment in his classroom to a more conducive PBL classroom. Jacob moved his teacher desk into the middle of the room. He got rid of all his student desks and replaced them with tables from around the school or with standing tables that he built himself. Jacob began to have a better understanding as to why these methods had to go and why PBL was a necessity in his classroom. PBL is not your typical "Here's your project, here's your rubric, and this (shows class an example) is what you're creating" type of project. It's identifying a problem or challenge and investigating ways to find an authentic solution. Jacob likes to use the analogy with his students that he's in the backseat riding along on their journey. He doesn't know the destination and he's okay if they take the scenic route. There will be times of heavy traffic and terrible storms to drive through, but he's only there for the conversation. He can't do the driving for them. They need to drive their way through these obstacles and setbacks and take him to their destination. Each student has their own destination they're driving him toward.

This PBL project that Jacob implemented involved having the students participate in creating new legislation law for the school. Jacob and his students started with the idea that the twenty-first-century school environment needs to adapt to the needs of its current students. Jacob had students write down a word they would use to describe school, and they posted them on the wall. Once the groups identified their system of government, they began to work together on passing new legislation and creating an environment that is more conducive to their twenty-first-century learning styles. Since this PBL was attached to their constitution unit, they identified how laws and "change" are created through a legislative process and how, in a school system, the students are part of the legislative branch because they represent the school population. The groups then decided on "the branches" of a school system and how the accountability and checks and balances occur within a school system. By talking to staff, students, administration, and the community, they were able to create a new school constitution. Students realized that they have a voice in the decisions that are made in school. They realized that the process to pass new legislation can be lengthy yet worth it in the end. Jacob conducted small interviews throughout the process to assess their reasoning for their legislation law. It all needed to come back to solving their driving question. About halfway through the project, they completed an elevator pitch to the class who then critiqued the gaps and cracks and some ideas that might need to be added.

Ideas for change in their schools ranged from block scheduling to 1:1 Chromebooks for students. From adding in school pep rallies to changing over to washable plastic trays in the cafeteria to help the environment. From adding vending machines to how they utilize and assign homework. Each group brought a unique idea to the table for change. They of course needed to identify the reasons and research behind why and how these changes would make school a better experience. The class took their findings and research and went on a field trip to central office. Their school superintendent took time out of his day to take each of Jacob's classes through the central office and speak with district directors. Jacob was very proud of how his students presented their research to these school leaders with such confidence.

Fast-forward two months later and the students have realized that they have a voice in their schools. At the middle school level, they will begin the 2018 school year with each student receiving their own Chromebook. They've added three additional technology electives for students to choose from. They'll be giving their media center a twenty-first-century makeover and creating a Makerspace. And most importantly, students are being included in the decision-making process for *their* school!

There were certainly some setbacks throughout the project too. Some of them were just speed bumps, but some of the students were running their cars off the road entirely! It was difficult for them to wrap their minds around not knowing exactly how to navigate their way through a project without having that model in front of them to re-create. But Jacob assured them he would always be there to help them along the way. After teaching for seventeen years, Jacob has realized that the needs of students are best measured by the students themselves. Not the teachers, not the administration, and certainly not the individuals at central office.

PBL is not just a change in the way educators meet their students' needs. It's a change in the mind-set of every educator. It's letting go of certain areas of control in your classroom and trusting the process and your students to find solutions on their own. Be okay with taking risks and failing because it only creates more opportunities for you to learn and grow as an educator. It models to your students that it's okay to take risks and fail. Because when our cars break down, we don't scrap them. We get them fixed and back on the road again. It's the only way we'll make it to our destination.

Aaron Sebens

Central Park School for Children, Durham NC, 4th-grade teacher
14 years teaching experience
Our Solar-Powered Classroom

Five years ago, Aaron Sebens came up with the idea of taking his classroom off the grid by using solar power. He used Kickstarter to raise money. It ended up going viral. He actually raised more money than what was needed for the initial idea. He scaled up, involved a lot of community stakeholders, and made it happen. It was amazing to see the community support the class also had with the involvement from the coffee shop next door donating a dollar a drink to the solar project. Five years later, his classroom is still running off solar and wind energy. The Department of Energy made a video about their project, and President Obama even tweeted about it.[21]

The students monitor the electricity production and consumption daily. Students learn all the components of the solar-powered system and give tours to other students and parents. They also compete in a wind turbine engineering and design contest every year. A 5kW grid-tied system was installed at the middle school in their community, and they are using the dividends from it to provide microloans to green energy projects around the world.

One very incredible opportunity this project produced was one that Aaron will never forget. The class learned about some musicians, Tim O'Brien and Darrell Scott, who had written a Grammy-nominated song about clean energy called "Keep Your Dirty Lights On." The class reached out to them and asked if they wanted some fourth-grade-backup singers when they came to town, and sure enough they did! Aaron's class got to sing a few songs with them on stage in front of a few thousand people.[22] Talk about an amazing opportunity for a group of fourth graders to get excited and passionate about a real-world topic! One student, a mandolin player, even got to play a solo during this concert and brought down the house. He also got to do a radio show with them at another festival they attended.

The amazing aspect of this project, as Aaron has witnessed, is that students aren't just learning about what electricity is, they are creating it, using it, and monitoring it every day.

It has made Aaron more engaged and passionate about what he teaches, and he's learned that a big project like this is a tool to open doors to communities around the world and change the trajectory of what students think *they* can do.

Go to THEPBLPLAYBOOK.com for more resources, materials, and guiding questions about this chapter.

CHAPTER 13:

PBL to Drive Choice and Learner Agency

XOXXOXOOXO

Kalli Colley

South Marshall Middle School; teacher

6 years of teaching experience

Shark Tank—Unit Title: Entrepreneurship: Collaboration, Creativity, and the Art of Persuasion

In this project based on the hit show *Shark Tank*, Kalli Colley has her students collaborate to create an original business or product. Throughout the project, they will research product development and competition, financial aspects of business, advertising, and other business principles. They will read both nonfiction and fiction in order to learn more about innovation, entrepreneurs, and the benefits and downfalls of technology.

The intended outcome for students is a business or product complete with a business plan or prototype, visual aid, and presentation that they will present to a panel of "sharks" composed of teachers, administration, and community members (specifically, community members who own a business or work in a financial field; these people can offer real-world feedback to students). The "sharks" will judge their work based on their creativity, cooperation, critical thinking skills, presentation skills, diplomacy when answering questions, and the product's projected success in society. Students will make a "deal" with an investor.

Students are graded on the business itself, the process of brainstorming and collaborating with their group, their presentation skills, and other written assignments concerning the project. Investments and feedback from the "sharks" will have no impact on their grades whatsoever. Grades are determined through rubrics completed by Kalli throughout the entire project. The project was initially completed individually or in partners. Now, it is completed in groups of four to encourage collaboration.

At the beginning of the project, Kalli and her students watch an episode of *Shark Tank* to hook students and talk about innovation and persuasive strategies. After that, students take a "True Colors" personality assessment, which splits them into four groups based on leadership and personality traits (orange, blue, gold, and green). Students may choose groups but must have one of each color in their group. Kalli and her students talk about successful collaboration and how to communicate with different personality types. Then, students begin brainstorming ideas for their business. After everyone has submitted their idea through a "classroom patent application" and have been approved for an original idea, they begin working on a business plan, prototype, advertisement, logo, and pitch. There are several milestone deadlines through the project to make sure they are progressing appropriately.

At the end, students present and negotiate with sharks. Kalli has used a variety of different personalities for her "sharks" that she says adds to the "realness" of the project. One of her coworkers, a science teacher and avid cynic, is known as the "tough" shark who really asks them hard questions but gives great feedback. One of her social studies teachers loves to overdramatize and say things like "I don't normally do this, but I'm going to roll the dice on you" and has been known to go out in the hallway to make phone calls to "ask his banker" or "consult with co-investors." Kalli's school secretary and guidance counselor have been sharks for her every year and have "invested" in many of the businesses that have been presented. Her administrators (in school and from the board office) look forward to seeing the ideas and jumping in to be a part of the fun. Community members including insurance salesmen, HR managers, entrepreneurs, bankers, store owners, and photographers have all come and given their feedback using their personal experience in the real world as well as their personalities. Presentation days are hectic and sometimes stressful but are her favorite part of the whole project. Each shark has an imaginary sum of $500,000 per class period to invest in businesses. They give feedback just like the show and complete surveys on each group. Kalli gives awards to the groups that earn the most money for their "first year of sales" based on an equation she uses involving their rubrics and investments. Kalli uses a rubric for each milestone assignment, a rubric for their ability to work collaboratively, and a rubric for the final presentation.

Kalli believes that because of this PBL project, her students research and read informational texts more diligently. They are more confident in their presentations and answering questions because they feel like they have ownership and are invested in their ideas. They think out of the box and get excited about innovation and collaboration. This project is truly cross-curricular, and even students who don't usually enjoy reading class find themselves engaged.

Kalli says that one major struggle each year seems to always be the brainstorming process for students. It is difficult for them to come up with an original idea. She understands that it's a lot to ask, but she really wants to see how groups do under this kind of pressure. How do they think through the problem? How do they overcome the feeling of "everything has already been invented?"

Kalli asserts that even if you don't feel creative, there are plenty of resources out there to try—find one that interests you and modify it to fit your classroom and your students. PBL doesn't have to be *all* nontraditional. There will be elements of traditional teaching scattered throughout group work, research, videos, and more. The opportunities are endless.

Lynn Cashell

Bethel Springs Elementary School
22 years of teaching experience
Alphabet Books

Lynn Cashell's fourth-grade students created an alphabet book for a specific audience using their own choice of topic and audience. The books could be created electronically using a variety of digital formats or on paper. This project was linked into her nonfiction reading and writing units and covers standards in reading, writing, grammar, research, and technology. The students were given complete choice of topic and audience, plus the digital or nondigital platform they wanted to use for publishing. Students shared their finished books in the library, with the intended audiences in their classrooms, with their class peers, and with friends and family via Seesaw.

The engagement and level of knowledge gained about their topics were very high. The students also learned how to navigate a variety of digital platforms, discovering and sharing what they learned with others. The students could not wait to share their final products with their classmates, audiences, and parents. Given a "regular" nonfiction writing assignment, Lynn had not seen this level of investment, collaboration, or excitement.

Lynn continually set up conferences with students throughout the writing and researching processes. She created a combination of a Genius Hour and GRIT rubric to assess their process and knowledge. Lynn was able to see the strength of empowering students though choice. They were not only writing for her, their teacher, but an authentic audience. Experiencing their level of investment and excitement caused Lynn to realize the power of a PBL activity. Her favorite interchange with students is when they ask "Can I . . ." and she answers "Why not?" She has let go of many of her preconceived notions of being the Sage on the Stage, to being a Guide on the Ride. Lynn truly believes that the most important thing to offer is student choice. The project still has structure, but lots of fluidity within it is based on the students' interests.

Tara Irani

Holy Trinity School, Richmond Hill, Ontario, High School Chemistry
11 years of teaching experience
Chemicals Rule the World!

This particular PBL project has evolved over the years. Initially it started with Tara Irani's previous department head. They wanted to make a more meaningful assignment for their students covering quite a few curriculum expectations. So in its original state, it was less robust. Tara's school is very much in favor of personalizing student learning in the form of more rich, larger-scale projects. In August 2017, Tara attended a PBL workshop at Hillfield Strathallan College offered by the Buck Institute. That is where she took the current project to the next level and basically redesigned it from what she had originally to its current status. When Tara came back to school in September, she discussed everything with her teaching partner, and together they put together the project framework and rolled it out to their students.

Students were required to discuss both qualitative and quantitative components of their element and compound. Concepts needed to include the structure of element/compound, their properties, the type of bonding and reactions involved, the amounts of reactants and products needed to form your compound, and how the structure helps determine the compound's properties. Students needed to explain how the compound properties help suit it to the job(s) people commonly use the chemical for. Students would evaluate the safety of the chemical by analyzing both its potential benefits and its potential risks to human health and/or the environment. Students also needed to recommend guidelines for the safe use of the chemical (e.g., suggest ways to reduce any harmful effects and suggest safer alternative chemicals that can do the same job).

Tara is a big believer in putting curriculum in context for her students so that it can provide real meaning and application for them. The grade-11 chemistry course lends itself nicely to a project-based approach by allowing students to connect what they learn in class and apply it to an element and compound they are curious to learn more about.

As Tara has learned through her PBL workshops and personally relating these ideals to her students, she says to keep an open mind about PBL. Take something that you are currently working on and build on it to make it a richer experience for your students. Be prepared to make changes along the way and be flexible.

Rebecca Chambers

John McCrae SS Ottawa ON, Teacher
15 years of teaching experience
Human Issue Inquiry

Rebecca Chambers's students are asked to pick a current issue that they are passionate about and are interested in learning about that relates to Human Growth and Development throughout the Lifespan.

The purpose of the inquiries is to learn and become an expert about a current issue, relate it to the curriculum, and promote and create awareness for the issue, all while working on exit outcomes. Students are expected to constantly be asking themselves questions such as "What is the issue today? How does someone cope with this issue? How do they rise above it?"

The students' job for each inquiry is to make their friends, family, John McCrae community, Barrhaven, Ottawa, Ontario, Canada, and the world aware of the issue that they hopefully have become passionate about. Students learn about social entrepreneurship and how social media can be used as a vehicle for social change. In order to successfully promote and share their knowledge of the current issue that they are looking at, they are required to post their findings on social media as well as get their media product out to as many people that will listen.

At the beginning of the project, each student works with Rebecca or a guest teacher to create an action plan, and it is placed on a whiteboard in the classroom with check boxes. They are required to check in with that each day. Students receive weekly feedback on their social media posts; since they are all working on different issue, this gives Rebecca the opportunity to see what they are working on or not working on and making sure that they are hitting curriculum expectations. Students also use a "Tweet Sheet" to place their tweets into curriculum categories so that they can make sure that they are covering their curriculum expectations. As students work away at their projects, Rebecca tries to check in with each of them to see if they need help. At the end of the project, students are required to reflect on the process. This is when Rebecca really tries to get them to see that it is the most important part. At the end of the reflection, students are required to give themselves an overall mark. Rebecca will look at the mark that they have given themselves and have a discussion with them explaining why she agrees or disagrees with them, and they mutually come up with their mark.

A few examples of the students' products are found on YouTube.[23]

At the end of each semester, Rebecca asks her students to give her feedback on how they think things went. Here were two of her favorite responses:

What was also satisfying for me was the ability to learn and research whatever we wanted. I find that learning things you want to learn produces better work because it's always interesting to research for it. I enjoyed having the freedom to go in my own direction with the inquiries but still have sort of a guideline to follow. I also think though it was satisfying that each unit we always did an inquiry so I would always know what to improve on or what to do next unit to make it better because I could compare it to the feedback on the previous inquiry. (Grade-12 student)

I found it very satisfying once I finished the inquiry and was able to have something to show for all my hard work. I also found it satisfying that I was able to remember what I learned from the different units as opposed to a lot of courses where everything is learned so fast it's hard to remember. (Grade-12 student)

Rebecca is adamant that change is necessary in the school systems. She believes that we ask students to take risks, to put themselves out there, and to try new things, and if things go wrong make sure you persevere and keep going—teachers need to take their own advice! It can be scary and messy at first, but in the end, it is very worth it!

Randy Thompson

Menahga, MN, Middle School Teacher
10 years of teaching experience
Pre-Algebra Driving Question Connections

In Randy Thompson's class, students come up with a driving question and then relate the standards to their driving question. His students have around 20% of their class time devoted to relating the standards and lessons to their driving question. Students create a portfolio that has each lesson relating to helping them solve their driving question. The project ends with a TED-style presentation that is filmed, complete with an audience and spotlights. Since his project runs simultaneous with his curriculum, Randy is assessing the content knowledge during the other 80% of classwork time. At the end of the project, students are scored upon completing each lesson as well as their presentation.

Randy knows PBL is directly tied to the increased student engagement, increased grades, and increased test scores he's seen. He also does surveys with the students. These results are a wonderful tool in stepping back and seeing how the project related to each individual student.[24]

Randy remembers a student he had the first year who really shined. She was new to the school and quite shy. One of her friends from childhood had passed away from a four-wheeling accident, and she decided to research and find ways to improve safety in four-wheeling. She didn't mention her friend's experience until halfway through the project (two months later). Randy then began to see the passion that she had for the project. Her "best five minutes of her life" presentation was amazing, and the class was extremely inspired. She was one of the first students to do this project for Randy and still is one of his favorites to this day. Last year on teacher-appreciation week, she wrote Randy a note that read: "Mr. Thompson, I remember my first day of seventh grade at a new school, walking into your classroom. I was so scared and I wasn't even sure I was in the right classroom. I am so thankful that you made seventh grade not as scary as I thought it was going to be. I had a ton of fun! Thank you!" In thinking about this student, Randy knows that she was born with confidence, but the PBL project in pre-algebra allowed her to develop it even more. Now just last month, she was one of the few female participants in the world famous Beargrease Dog Sled Marathon.

Randy explains that PBL has had a tremendous impact on his career. He was on a team of teachers that his district allowed to meet once a day during two consecutive school years. Their task was to find a way to make learning more meaningful to their specific students. Randy's team landed on project-based learning after visiting other schools in Minnesota as well as doing other research. This then impacted Randy individually where he did his Master's Action-Research on PBL. This has carried over into his teaching and has influenced the other subjects that he teaches as well. You can see examples of his students' work in some of his YouTube videos ("Thompson052312").[25]

The first year was indeed quite a struggle for Randy because he knew what he wanted in his head, but it was hard to translate that to his students. He didn't have any examples to show. Now in his third year of this semester project, Randy is able to pick his best examples to show, and students have a better understanding of the expectations. "The cool part about PBL," Randy says, "is that at the end of a 20% Time class period, your head will hurt in a unique way that you'll never otherwise experience as a teacher."

Anthony Babington Blackhurst

St. Peter's Girls School, South Africa
47 years of teaching experience
Mr. B's Game of Life

Anthony Babington Blackhurst believes PBL is a modern label for things many educators who do not provide education "in straightjackets" have been doing for many years. He taught under an "integrated day" system in the 1970s, and he's always believed pupils learn best if they are inquisitive and teach themselves and one another.

Anthony's "Mr. B's Game of Life" project is essentially the growth and management of a town on a 2.5 meter by 1 meter board. Aspects of business, elections, taxation, talent shows, medical-aid practices, classroom duties, and the like are integrated. He has played this game for seventeen years, and no two years are ever run the same way. Sometimes it runs for a third of the year, sometimes for the whole year. The students always know and can do much more at the end of the game than at the beginning.

Anthony explains that all his pupils do something he calls E and L: Exploration and Learning. This E and L are similar to PBL. A group of teachers is assigned to all year groups for such exercises, and sometimes pupils engage with one another across grades. Anthony adjusts his methods every year and has always done so. He places emphasis on pupils' learning and teaches as little as absolutely necessary.

Anthony's advice is to learn by reading, listening, experimenting, and sharing. Make each child the center of a slightly different learning process. Let the child have an input into his/her own learning direction and see purpose in it. Make learning hands-on and practical.

Go to THEPBLPLAYBOOK.com for more resources, materials, and guiding questions about this chapter.

CHAPTER 14:

PBL Taking Research to the Next Level

XOXXOXOOXO

Patrice Becicka

College Community School District
20 years of teaching experience
How Do We Know? The Junk Detective

Through professional learning with her district, Patrice Becicka became very interested in alternate ways to engage her students rather than traditional teaching strategies. Throughout her teaching career, she has always looked for ways to get kids engaged at higher levels. Patrice decided to try PBL. She was already dabbling in elements of it anyway through gamification. When she attended conferences and took the opportunity to learn more, she was introduced to the PBL Starter kit book, and it changed her teaching. Patrice began writing her own PBLs based on the formats found in the book *Project Based Learning (PBL) Starter Kit* by John Larmer, David Ross, and PhD John R. Mergendoller.

For Patrice's Junk Detective unit, students applied historical thinking skills, along with literacy skills to re-create an "ancient civilization" (present day will represent the ancient civilization). Each student synthesized their knowledge of the work of an archaeologist. For this project, the students used role-play; each of them became an archaeologist assistant for "Howard Carson" from the book *Motel of the Mysteries* by David Macaulay. As they worked through the project, each student maintained a hard copy assistant's journal. Patrice adds that she implemented anecdotal evidence, their archaeologist notebook that they kept throughout the unit, and a conference with an authentic audience (adults outside of the school building sat down with two students at a time and had a conference with them about their learning, completing a rubric for feedback as well as verbal feedback). The students were much more engaged in their learning. Patrice was so excited by the amount of learning the kids were able to share when it was their turn. They presented their "archaeology field journals," shared pictures from their "digs," and used correct terminology/vocabulary terms. They had been active learners and at parent-teacher conferences they were able to go into great detail about the unit, their learning, and their final projects.

Patrice says that PBL has reenergized her teaching. She loves watching the kids get so involved in and take ownership over their learning. She reminds new PBL users to be prepared for anything. Allow for students to take the learning in a direction you did not anticipate and be flexible. In fact, the only struggle Patrice says she had was to keep up with the kids. They wanted more and more information. She learned to stay out of their way!

Parthena Savides

Central Christian Academy, 4th-grade teacher
4 years of teaching experience
Medieval Story Project

The specific question this project addresses is "What was life like in the medieval period?" After hooking the children that they will be creating and designing their own story, Parthena Savides and her students discuss what they would need to research in order to get an understanding of that period. They then do the research and create a story with it. After researching, they present their findings and story line to the class for feedback. They are responsible for creating props, costumes, drawings, or whatever else they need to bring their story to life. Within their story, they need to include medieval weapons that discuss force and motion. As Parthena and her class discuss fractions and adding fractions, they then build their own trebuchets incorporating fractions with the measurements to build the frame and the science of force and motion to actually launch it. Each of their stories must have a visual aspect to share on the Internet. In the past, the students have just done movies, but this year, Parthena is giving them the choice of how they want to create that story. It could be a movie, radio show, online storybook, or another form that they can create on their own.

Parthena has noticed that the children are much more engaged when they get to work on projects like this, especially aspects that encourage their creativity. They are more eager, and the pride in their work is much more evident than a simple quiz or test's demonstration of knowledge. Parthena gives them checkpoints throughout the project to make sure that they stay on top of their work. Students who do not meet the checkpoint have points taken off. In the end, the final product is evaluated based on a rubric as well as a writing sample that gives an opportunity for the children to explain how and why they did certain things within their story.

Many examples come to mind when Parthena contemplates how PBL has helped certain students come out of their shell and go above and beyond their norm. Her favorite story is one student who chose to play an evil character even though it is the complete opposite of his true self. This is a child who never gets angry, but he got angry in the video as the evil Baron Von Rumpelstiltskin. When the video was shown to his classmates, they all thought it was amazing and hilarious. His parents later told Parthena that he had taken the DVD of his movie on a vacation to show the entire extended family and all his friends; they thought he was quite a star, not to mention how proud he was of his performance.

One struggle Parthena does have is being able to find iPads for the children to use to be able to edit their videos on their own. In the past, Parthena had edited the videos—that was no doubt an overwhelming task to try to complete along with all the other responsibilities of being a teacher. She contemplated quitting the project, and later, her principal came and talked to her about continuing because it was such a quality project-based learning experience. Parthena decided to change the project by having the students work in groups to create the story and its entire production. Now she has to worry only about securing four iPads to edit green-screen footage. She continues to discuss with her colleagues and principal ways to facilitate the access of additional technology, and she hopes that can be accomplished at some point as this year the students' energy is even more contagious, and the parts that they were more excited to research are showing up in their projects (example: the food of the medieval period as they create a medieval cooking show).

Overall, Parthena knows she could not continue teaching if she could not use the PBL method. Growing up, she wondered why teachers did not teach in a way that connected all the subjects. When in graduate school for teaching, she was introduced to interdisciplinary studies and through that, project-based learning. Parthena was so excited that this type of learning very much coincided with how she wanted to teach when she was a child. She loves that the children never look like they are about to fall asleep but have sparkles in their eyes. Over the years of doing project-based learning, Parthena is always taken aback by the creativity of the children as they think through the problems and design the parts of their project in ways that she would not have thought of. Parthena realizes that after experiencing the joy of project-based learning, she could never go back to a more traditional classroom.

Eventually, Parthena was able to find the four iPads that she needed mostly from parents being willing for the child to bring in his or her personal iPad for school use. Parthena loved that the students did their own movies, and she could tell that the kids were even more proud of them than in past years. She did a lesson about how authors set the mood of their stories through words and pictures; they then talked about how moviemakers set the tone—mostly through music. Parthena played a battle scene for them with different types of music to show how the scene changes because of the music. The students decided what the mood for each scene was. . . . Though they had a few technology glitches, they were able to present all four movies to the parents at their end-of-quarter event. Everyone was quite impressed with the work and the production of the students.

Susan Hedgcock

Sarasota Christian School; High School English Teacher
32 years of teaching experience
Your Turn: How Do You View History?

Susan Hedgcock uses the National History Day Theme: Conflict and Compromise to encourage her students to understand how to research and synthesize information and apply close-reading techniques in order to put together their view of history from a period and place that they have a connection with. This project is quite inclusive but covers individual standards for reading nonfiction and writing. She specifically aligned this project with the Reading Standards for Literacy in History/Social Studies 6–12 and Writing Standards for Literacy in History/Social Studies. This unit can also apply to social studies classes, with the appropriate standards and English classes with the general standards for information texts, language, speaking, listening, and writing. Students are also given the standards in the form of competencies in "I can" statements and asked to assess their level of understanding and support their choices. They also confer on these and arrive at an agreement with this decision. This is what Susan records in her SBG gradebook.

Before Susan applied PBL, she had an organized system with checkpoints that limited the pathway to accomplishing the task. She provided topic areas as well. The purpose of the project was to specifically teach research, the *Chicago* style of annotation, and writing a paper. The only choice involved was which topic the student would choose and how the topic was developed.

Susan spends more time teaching and empowering students to be a part of the design. She uses TED Talks, such as, "Getting Out of the Box, Thinking Creatively." She also spends time using Stanford History Group's "Reading Like a Historian" to teach the skills and approach to understanding history. Susan creates a scenario where they are detectives or they are commissioned as historians to tell the story and then they have a framework to make choices.

Susan spends time guiding students on how to approach history in order to help them with the decision-making process so that they can find their unique interests, rather than be influenced by the teachers.

She also spends more time teaching and encouraging student reflection, rather than teacher feedback. Students choose the format to presenting their research, rather than just a paper. They can design an exhibit, documentary, performance, website, or paper. Students also present to an authentic audience to make their case for their historic claims. This gives them a sense of mission and purpose.

Susan often finds herself in the role of coach and facilitator, the student's "concierge." She loves playing this role and finds that her relationship with students has truly become that of a mentor. The projects and academic work that students produce are far superior to anything generated in the past. Students become experts in their research, and their understanding is much deeper. They are more resourceful in their learning, and they are more independent. They are self-directed.

When it comes to PBL, Susan explains that once you teach them how to fly, they will not be satisfied with the conventional classroom. Students are taught how to reflect at every stage of their project. This becomes the central tool used to assess. Susan conferences with students when they are ready and keeps a checklist, so everyone has a touch point with her daily.

Today, Susan admits that she looks at learning and assesses outcomes differently. So many soft skills are enhanced by this approach, such as taking responsibility for one's actions, collaboration, trust, and persistence. In fact, this approach helps to develop a growth mind-set and establish a positive learning culture in her classroom. She reminds educators to trust the silence. Sometimes educators are too impatient and expect students to immediately shift into gear and go. Too many times Susan has seen the struggle itself create the best learning experience.

Nathan Kraai

Oak Hill School-Nashville, TN—Tech Integrator and Makerspace Coordinator
11 years of teaching experience
Ancient Egyptian Museum

This was done with a sixth-grade social studies class because the classroom teacher had the passion to teach in more powerful ways. Nathan Kraai brought this idea to the teacher, and fortunately, she trusted him enough to give up valuable instruction time for him to teach this project. Students studied various civilizations up until the decline of the Roman Empire. Ancient Egypt and surrounding Mesopotamia is a civilization that is studied deeply. Students learn about geography, religion, architecture, the origins of writing, etc. Nathan took this particular PBL unit and added the museum feature as the primary driver of content understanding. No longer was the teacher in charge of teaching students about the different parts of the Ancient Egyptian culture, but the charge was on the students to teach each other about these cornerstones of the culture.

The challenge or problem that Nathan proposed to his students was this: How can you design a museum exhibit that would fit into a larger Egyptian exhibit that conveys your learning about one specific topic? (architecture or hieroglyphics, for instance). The challenge went deeper as students were forced to think about how to design this exhibit for somebody else. Using the design process, students developed and interviewed other students to gauge how they would want to learn at a museum. On top of this, they were also forced to figure out how to design this exhibit so that learning could occur even if the students who created the exhibit were not present.

As for assessments, Nathan utilized a combination of a maker framework (creative confidence, initiative, effort, etc.) along with a rubric focused on assessing the different stages of design thinking. At the end, students were asked to write a reflection on the entirety of the project and the learning derived from it.

Nathan has learned that the greatest thing about these types of projects is that every student can have a voice, and it can be "heard" in a variety of different ways. Students who are often quiet or disengaged in a traditional classroom setting now have the opportunity to share their creativity and ideas in ways they haven't been able to do before. Those kids who are better at building and creating are leaned upon heavily in the group setting to help develop the prototype or final product. PBL gets all kids involved in ways that they want to be involved.

Nathan admits, as many do, that his biggest struggle in implementing PBL is dedicating enough time in order to accomplish the project successfully. Being a new project, he was unsure of the amount of time that would be required to complete the project. So near the end, the kids were rushing because of the deadline. However, Nathan had so many kids asking to come in before school, work during lunch, or want to stay after school because they were fully invested in what they were doing. Many kids told him that they asked for hot glue guns as Christmas presents because they loved the opportunity to demonstrate their knowledge in hands-on ways.

Nathan states that when he first started teaching, he measured the success he was having based on the success his students would have on assessments and standardized tests. They may have been learning the content, but it was done artificially and without joy, passion, or wonder. As Nathan has implemented PBL, he's come to see the power of authentic challenges that stir the creativity within each student and force kids to wrestle with the content they are being asked to learn. Kids are no longer off task, no longer saying something is boring, and going above and beyond the expectations rather than simply meeting them and moving on.

Brandon Bogumil

St. Timothy's School Raleigh, NC Imagination Lab Teacher
5 years of teaching experience
Native American and NC Settler's Dwellings

At St. Timothy's School, fourth-grade students learn about Native American, Moravian, and Mountain Settlements in North Carolina in the seventeenth century. The teachers have been trying to develop a project related to this unit in which the students use the knowledge to produce something, and Brandon Bogumil came up with the idea of the students, working in groups, designing a community building for the settlements. They have to use only available resources at the time, and it has to meet the needs of the community.

Before PBL, the students produced a PowerPoint presentation about the settlements. That evolved to an Animoto, and then Brandon approached the teachers about designing a community building. As this is a community building they are developing, they have to synthesize a lot of information to understand what their settlement's community would need and want from a community building. Students are much more engaged and focused. It feels fun, like real learning, and less like school.

The students make models of the buildings after designing them, and the models use the actual materials, on a smaller scale, which is exciting for the students when they share their work with the rest of the class. One such student Brandon remembers impressed him greatly when it came to the presentation component. He was able to speak very well about his creation and explained it inside out while showing a deep understanding of the techniques the Native American tribe used to build their homes. He was a student that struggled at times with articulating ideas when doing work, so to see his confidence in his understanding of the topic and ability to articulate was extremely rewarding to Brandon. On the other hand, some of the students really struggled with physically realizing their ideas when building a model out of paper, foam, pipe cleaners, Popsicle sticks, and other fabrication materials available. Brandon also found that a lot of students struggled with collaboration when they had to work as a group to come up with one idea that represented all their contributions and not just a few dominant personalities.

Brandon had his share of challenges as well. The first was in developing the project. He knew he wanted to create personas for the students to look at, so he could simulate the students interacting with clients as an architect would. When Brandon sat down to do this, he realized he did not have the historical knowledge to make them authentic, so a lot of research had to be done. The second challenge was during the implementation. The students were struggling in working collaboratively, and after much thought on why, Brandon realized that the problem rested on his shoulders. He had not actually taught them how to work together in this way, having had just thrown them into it. This changed his approach to collaborative work, and he realized that the students needed to be taught how to work together.

Brandon explains that each of the teachers involved had different ways of assessing. There are definitely a lot of informal assessments as the students work through the process. What Brandon found with PBL is that the students tend to voice the fact that they are not progressing because they want to move forward to complete the work. This helps him facilitate their growth and work with them as a partner and serve them as a resource. When the student is able to stand up, share their model, and tell the story of how and why it was created, it is very obvious whether they are developing the skills Brandon and his colleagues want them to develop.

As many PBL educators will tell you, Brandon's advice is to start small. Start with one project in your curriculum, and make sure it is open-ended, and you do not have a product in mind. Let the students take control and create. It is scary and can be frustrating, but you need to trust the students and realize that the first time will be messy and you won't necessarily feel extremely happy afterward, but in reflection, it will get easier and easier. Let it grow naturally and organically. It is worth it.

Jon Tobergte

Sycamore Community Schools, 5th-Grade Language Arts Teacher
5 years of teaching experience
Spinner Debate

For this project, Jon Tobergte had students research the pros and cons of using spinners in school. Students picked a side and gathered evidence to prove their case. Following that, students joined a debate team and debated in front of a panel of judges that included a variety of people (superintendent, board member, administration, and teachers). Whatever the judges decided would become the policy of the team. This project fulfilled several research standards, presentation standards, and text evidence standards and included opinion writing, and reading rigorous leveled texts.

Student level of engagement was incredibly high, and their passion for learning was more evidence than Jon has ever seen. Students developed a critical eye for good evidence versus bad evidence. He used a research data sheet, and students wrote a "brief" for their debates. They also assessed their knowledge through debate presentations. Jon has now realized the importance of allowing student voice and choice in his projects; making learning mean something to the kids makes all the difference.

There have been many, many success stories thus far. One student, in particular, happens to be a low-achieving student who is also on free and reduced lunch. This is a student who struggles daily academically. She was put into a group where one of the other students was a very, very bright student but struggles with the English language and has emotional issues that get in the way of his success at school on a daily basis. One day, the student who struggles emotionally had completely shut down (this happens often). The other student came to Jon for help, and he told her that he had "specifically" chosen her for her patience and determination to work with this student and that she was to be the leader of the group. The student looked unsure of herself but went back to the group and immediately began encouraging the emotionally challenged student to get into the work. She would say things like "I know you can do this. You are so smart, and we need you." She would tell him "great job" and "we are making progress." Within a half hour, the emotionally struggling student had a smile and had produced an entire page of writing, which had not been seen from him the entire year. The low-achieving student could not believe how great of a job she had done. Jon gave her an award and acknowledged her in front of all her peers as being the leader he always thought she could be.

Another one of Jon's students struggles with reading fluently so much so that she can be tough to listen to. With the debates, Jon was very worried about how she might perform being that she struggles with reading in general. He wondered how she would sound for her group when presenting. However, what she produced was unlike anything Jon had seen from her before. She spoke loudly, fluently, and with great confidence. She was definitely the most surprising performance he had and was a big reason why her team made it all the way to the semifinals.

The struggle Jon has encountered with this project is the amount of planning time. PBL projects take more time than he expected. He plans with his team every day for at least an hour a day, many days up to two hours. They have been able to take a full school day just to plan on top of that. Grouping the students in different ways presents some challenges as well because students work differently with different students. They also have many different ability levels. It is also a challenge to involve all four subjects into a PBL unit. Finding common standards can be a tough task.

To sum it up in a short and sweet manner, Jon took the jump with PBL because his principal decided his team would be a good fit to try out the program. When he and his team researched it and tried it out, they never looked back.

Jesse Damiano

Warren Hills Regional High School—Biology Teacher, 10th grade
8 years of teaching experience
Is Your DNA Yours?

This PBL project directed by Jesse Damiano taught his students the makeup of DNA, and how it relates to genes and chromosomes. It explored the topic of ethics in terms of genetically designing humans. It began by having the students discuss whether they would send their DNA into companies such as 23andMe or AncestryDNA and what they would hope to get out of it. Jesse then passed out sample reports from 23andMe and had students answer questions about what information can be found in the report. Student then researched the companies and explained exactly what they do. As a class, students filled out a scaffold-type class data sheet with this research. Questions included: What is a genetic profile? What are genes? When we say "sequence of DNA" what does this mean? What exactly are the letters (ATCG) shown in an image of a strand of DNA? What patterns do you see with these letters? What are chromosomes? Students were also asked to add one question of their own and someone else must answer it.

Students completed a virtual lab on cloning plasmids to further understand how genetics can be bioengineered. Students then prepared for a formal debate about the ethical implications of companies like 23andme or AncestryDNA.

Students were assessed on their contributions to the shared Google document. They were also assessed using a rubric for the writing prompts and the debate.

Jesse attests to the fact that his career has drastically changed. He is no longer stressed when his students cannot remember the definition of terms that mean nothing to them. He finds his job so much more rewarding when his students can read a newspaper article about a topic and actually understand it because of the PBL they completed. He knows he is creating informed citizens, which is so important in today's world. His advice is a little different than others, but so very true. He says: "Don't get stuck on trying to find a PBL that someone else created. Go with your gut. Most times the one that someone else created is for *their* class. Your class is different. You know your students. Go with that and get creative."

Go to THEPBLPLAYBOOK.com for more resources, materials, and guiding questions about this chapter.

PART 3:
Becoming a PBL Designer—Taking Action to Create

CHAPTER 15:

PBL as a Path to Mastery

XOXXOXOOXO

In the fourteenth century, the term *genius* was regarded as a guardian spirit. Yet a person with "unworldly" talent was said to *have a genius*, because his/her gift (of genius) being a supernatural act. No one was said to *be a genius*, because that would quite literally mean you were a guardian spirit.

This changed in the 1600s, when the meaning began to morph and people would use the term *genius* to describe someone with natural ability, and someone with an exceptional natural capacity of intellect, not necessarily just a gift from a supernatural friend.

By the end of the seventeenth century, this usage was common, and the old terminology of *having a genius* seemed to fall out of the public vernacular. When you look at Google Ngram, the word *genius* was at its highest point of usage in the late 1700s and has been dropping in use steadily since the turn of the nineteenth century.

However, the word *genius* still resonates with people from various different cultures today. It conjures up images of Einstein, and we use it to describe contemporary leaders like Elon Musk. Elizabeth Gilbert—the author of *Eat, Pray, Love*—talks about this change in usage for *genius* during her very memorable TED Talk. She muses on the impossible things we expect from artists and geniuses—and brings back the idea that, instead of the rare person "being" a genius, all of us may "have" a genius.

The Start of Genius Hour

Now seven centuries later, and the term *genius* is being used by educators across the globe more than ever before. This is partly due to the explosion of *Genius Hour.* Genius Hour is a time given to students in classrooms around the world to work on inquiry-driven and passion-based projects that are built on intrinsic motivation.

I've been lucky enough to be a part of this movement, working with fantastic teachers and leaders who are letting students choose their learning path (if only for an hour a week). Other educators like Don Wettrick are taking this idea to the next level, writing in his book *Pure Genius* about his Innovation Class that uses this concept of inquiry-driven innovative work for an entire class period every day.

When I wrote *Inquiry and Innovation in the Classroom: Using 20% Time, Genius Hour, and PBL to Drive Student Success,* my thoughts were focused on bringing the creative and innovative power of learning back into our students' hands. I had seen what wonderful projects my students created when given this freedom to learn and make what they were interested in, as well as working with teachers like Joy Kirr, Hugh McDonald, Gallit Zvi, and Denise Krebs who were using Genius Hour to inspire students in the K-8 grades.

Now as this inquiry-driven movement moves forward into more and more classrooms across the country and the world, it is important to look at the impact of this kind of learning, as well as the ultimate goal for our students in exploring their passions with creative work.

The Hidden Problem with Creative Work

There are many people who see 20% Time and Genius Hour projects as complete freedom for students in the classroom. To an extent this is true.

Students have the freedom to work on a wide variety of interests and content, yet there are time constraints. There are usually some constraints on the scope of the project, how it is presented, and what the process often looks like as well.

This is why I've seen many teachers struggle their first time running an inquiry-driven project.

Freedom doesn't always lead to success. In fact, freedom is often one of the biggest factors for failure.

Students will struggle, and teachers will wonder why they are not excited to learn right away. **They forget that for many students, this is one of their first opportunities of true choice in their learning path, and they have rarely had this chance to explore their interests inside a school.** Other students are fired up to do work that matters but can't seem to bring it all together in a way that works.

I had one student of mine, Evan, proclaim to the entire class how he was going to sell 500 wristbands to raise money for a charity organization that he cared about during our *Project: Global Inform* inquiry-based group project. The passion was there for Evan. His heart was in the right place, and he set out to do this creative work of designing a unique wristband ("it's not going to be like those Livestrong bands, Mr. J") that would sell out quickly to his peers. Three days before the project was due, Evan finally received the wristbands. They didn't look right. He tried to sell them and wound up with under 100 sales by the time he had to present to the rest of the class.

Interestingly, here is where the learning took a turn. The problem with creative work is that it is often challenging to reach goals and find success. You'll have to fail many times before finding true success with most creative work. Evan stood up in front of the class and talked about his failures. His failure to design a wristband, his failure to manage the project, his failure to sell, and his ultimate failure to raise money for the organization he cared so much about. His classmates felt his pain. They too had failed at many of their creative projects. But then Evan said a line that made it all worth it:

"Even though I failed at almost every piece of this project, I feel like I still learned more in the past month than in almost any other time during school."

Failures are worth it when the goal is bigger than the task. Evan may have failed at this wristband idea, but he succeeded in learning.

Mastery Is the Goal. Learning Is the Habit.

Mastery is a process that we can work through and attain. Microtrials and failures play a huge role in mastery. Genius, on the other hand, seems to bring up the idea that either you have it . . . or you don't. It's why Genius Hour is so exciting because students get to play around with the notion that they are capable of great and wondrous creations, regardless of their age or abilities. Yet there is a problem with Genius being the goal.

Do not talk about giftedness, inborn talents! One can name great men of all kinds who were very little gifted. They acquired greatness, became "geniuses" (as we put it), through qualities the lack of which no one who knew what they were would boast of: they all possessed that seriousness of the efficient workman which first learns to construct the parts properly before it ventures to fashion a great whole; they allowed themselves time for it, because they took more pleasure in making the little, secondary things well than in the effect of a dazzling whole.

—Friedrich Nietzsche

The goal of the creative, passion-driven work our students are doing should be mastery. Mastering a concept, skill, or ability. It's silly to believe that one year of Genius Hour will lead to true mastery, but does it help? Does Genius Hour build good learning habits? Do those habits then eventually lead to mastery?

In Robert Greene's fantastic book *Mastery*, he weighs in on the imaginary wall we have crafted around people such as Einstein, DaVinci, and Edison:

Over the centuries, people have placed a wall around such mastery. They have called it genius and have thought of it as inaccessible. They have seen it as the product of privilege, inborn talent, or just the right alignment of the stars. They have made it seem as if it were as elusive as magic. But that wall is imaginary.[26]

In fact, as Greene points out in the book, all of these great "masters" who we refer to as "geniuses" followed a similar path to attain a level of mastery in their specific field.

First, they found and accepted their life's task. This is quite difficult. When parents, peers, and often teachers are telling students to follow a certain path . . . it makes it hard to truly listen to that inner voice pointing you in the direction that leads to a convergence of passion and purpose. This, too, is the first step of an inquiry-based project: choosing what you want to work on (and it is often the most difficult task).

Second, they had various forms of apprenticeship. They learned from other masters and improved their skills. In our world today, this does not always have to be a face-to-face apprenticeship. A good YouTube channel can serve as a mentor depending on your chosen field. Often this is where we tend to jump around. We'll get to this stage and go back to choosing a different task.

Greene mentions the impact of feeling intrinsically motivated: Our levels of desire, patience, persistence, and confidence end up playing a much larger role in success than sheer reasoning powers. Feeling motivated and energized, we can overcome almost anything. Feeling bored and restless, our minds shut off and we become increasingly passive.

Third, we must move on from the mentor to completely understand the field and all the social intelligence that comes with it.

This leads into the **fourth step, of creative and exploratory work.** You cannot become a true master by studying and taking tests. There has to be years of hard, agonizing, and often deflating work. That will be followed by moments of creative *genius,* as the world might describe it. Again, the merits of Genius Hour demonstrate how much more a student can learn when they are doing, making, and creating (even if they are failing in their current task).

When I look at Genius Hour, 20% Time, and other Project-Based Learning experiences, I see a strong connection to the steps to Mastery laid out in Greene's book.

I see students working to find a purpose in the work that they do. I've watched students struggle to come up with ideas that they could stick with and have seen what it looks like when a student is fueled by curiosity and an inner passion. I see failure as a part of the process to mastery and something to be celebrated during this time. I view apprenticeship (in its various forms) as a key piece to Genius Hour and any project. Finding a mentor (or mentors) is an area we should focus on even more when giving students the freedom to do creative work.

And finally, I see Genius Hour and PBL as a stepping-stone. It may not lead to a mastery while students are in school. But years later I can't wait to see what students will say about how their project-based learning and creative work in school led to them finding their life's task and becoming masters at whatever they set out to do in this world.

Go to THEPBLPLAYBOOK.com for more resources, materials, and guiding questions about this chapter.

CHAPTER 16:

Personalizing the PBL Experience

XOXXOXOOXO

Michael Port shares a story (in his book) about a donkey, an old man, and a boy:

> *An old man, a boy and a donkey were going to town. The boy rode on the donkey and the old man walked beside him. As they went along they passed some people who remarked it was a shame the old man was walking and the boy was riding. The man and boy thought maybe the critics were right, so they changed positions.*
>
> *Later, they passed some people who remarked, "What a shame! He makes that little boy walk." They then decided they would both walk.*
>
> *Soon they passed some more people who thought they were stupid to walk when they had a decent donkey to ride. So they both rode the donkey.*
>
> *Now they passed some people who shamed them by saying how awful to put such a load on a poor donkey. The boy and man said they were probably right, so they decided to carry the donkey. As they crossed the bridge, they lost their grip on the animal, and he fell into the river and drowned.*
>
> *The moral of the story? If you try to please everyone, you might as well kiss your ass goodbye.*[27]

Does this story remind you of your life right now as a teacher, administrator, parent, or educator? And yet, we know how important it is to personalize learning for our students. The research is loud and clear about choice and project-based learning opportunities. So how do we balance this?

What Is Personalized Learning?

First, I believe we need to understand the difference between personalized and individualized education. George Couros summed up the differences quickly in this post:

> *"Individualized" learning is having students go through different paths to get to the same end point. How you get there is different, but the destination is the same.*
>
> *"Personalized" learning is having students go through their own paths to whatever endpoint they desire. How you take the path and where you end up is totally dependent upon the strengths and interests of the learner.*[28]

While both are important to learning, let's focus on the latter for right now. In order to create and open up opportunities for *personalized learning*, a teacher must have a great deal of trust in what the learners will get out of this experience.

For many teachers, that is extremely difficult (it was for me as well). Having a specific curriculum and mapped-out guide of what students are going to learn, when they are going to learn it, how they will be measured and assessed, and then what intervention/remediation will be done after the assessment is easier to understand.

It's logical. It's a simple recipe to follow. And in many cases, it works.

But what happens when students don't want to follow that curriculum? What happens when they don't care about the subject? What happens when they are bored with the content and go through the motions? What happens when they are tired of *struggling* to find success on the same type of assessments?

Students, just like adults, need to feel some sense of ownership, autonomy, and purpose in order to have true engagement (read Daniel Pink's book *Drive* if you'd like to see more on this).

Blended learning. **Personalized** learning. **Individualized** learning. **Mass customized** learning. **Differentiated** learning. **Online** learning.

It seems we are obsessed with adding adjectives in front of the noun *learning*. While I have to believe this has been the case for a long time, it has picked up in steam over the past decade as technology has moved from being a learning event to an everyday part of our lives.

The problem with all these terms is that learning has always been personalized and individualized.

School, on the other hand, is an institution that in many cases advocates and sets up learning experiences to be common, compliant, and consistent.

This was never more apparent than when I was at the Learning and the Brain Conference a few weeks ago.

I was in a session where a teacher asked the presenter, "We are in a school that is implementing blended learning to create a more personalized learning experience for our students. But a big problem is that our curriculum focus has always been on Common Learning Experience for all students."

The presenter asked, *"What does common learning experience mean?"*

"Well, our focus is that if there were twins in my 6th-grade class, and my colleagues 6th-grade class, those twins would have the same learning experience every day, regardless of the teacher."

"Hmm," the presenter nodded. "Let me ask you a question, do you think any of us ever have the same learning experience? I mean, there are a lot of people in this room, but don't you think each will take away something every specific and individualized to their needs and their learning after today's session?"

The teacher smiled, "Yes, I see this every day as a teacher, and also with my own kids. Their experiences are always personalized!"

The dialogue brought the group to a big epiphany:

What if we focused our efforts on creating common learning quality, instead of common learning experiences?

If every learning experience is by definition, "personalized," why not focus on the quality instead of the same experience?

Learning Is a Personalized Experience

Last year I stumbled on the work of **Peter Nilsson**. I was blown away to see the science of learning made so clear. Nilsson is a teacher and school leader who works at Deerfield Academy in Massachusetts, and he has read extensively on the field of cognitive science. His 14-part series on "The Cognitive Science of Education" is a must-read for any educator (or parent) serious about understanding the way our brains process all this information we get each day.[29] This is serious. You need to go read the 14-part series. It should only take an hour or two at the most, but it may just be the most valuable time you spend as a teacher and learner.

Here is Peter Nilsson describing the four stages to learning on his blog, *Sense and Sensation*:

How People Learn:

Four cognitive processes every teacher should know

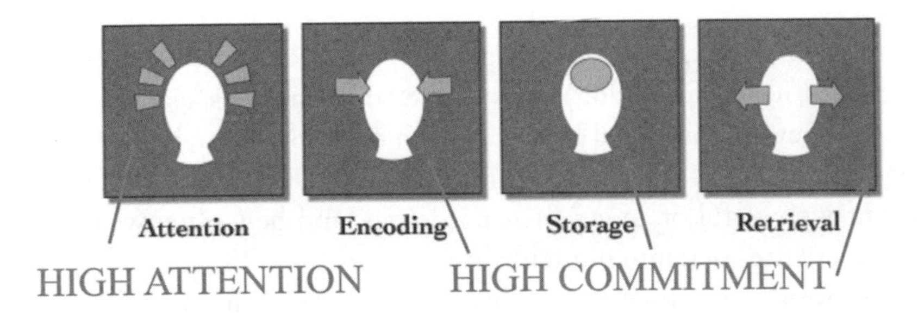

So how do people learn? What are the mechanics of memory? Can we distill thousands of articles and books to something that is manageable, digestible, and applicable to our classrooms?

Yes. In brief, the cognitive process of learning has four basic stages:

1. Attention: the filter through which we experience the world

2. Encoding: how we process what our attention admits into the mind

> *3. Storage: what happens once information enters the brain*
> *4. Retrieval: the recall of that information or behavior*
> *Almost everything we do or know, we learn through these stages, for our learning is memory, and the bulk of our memory is influenced by these four processes: what we pay attention to, how we encode it, what happens to it in storage, and when and how we retrieve it.*[30]

Let's start with **Attention**. Going back a previous idea on why we learn, it all begins with attention. Most of the time we pay attention for two reasons: interest or necessity.

Our brain is flooded with information from a multisensory world that is throwing sounds, sights, feelings, and everything else at us in rapid succession. With all this information coming at us, we tend to pay attention to things that we are curious and interested about, or information that has a direct correlation to our physical, emotional, or psychological well-being.

Then comes the **Encoding**. Our senses are being hit with so much information that when we finally process that information, we begin to categorize it as a new experience or a connected experience with prior knowledge.

After we've successfully paid attention and made some connections (or created new information), we come to the **Storage** stage. Here we store this new or connected information in our short-term, working, or long-term memory. Where it is stored and how it is stored is associated with how powerful of an experience it is/was, and how often we bring that experience back into our daily lives.

Retrieval is the final stage. This is when we pull information out of the memory to help us in learning something new, or adapting to a situation, or connecting the dots on an experience. Retrieval also allows us to "re-encode" which starts the learning process all over again. It's like a mini-version of the unlearning/relearning cycle we discussed in the last article.

You can think about how this cycle of learning works in all different types of contexts and experiences. From real-world applications like driving a car, to classroom situations like understanding photosynthesis, the more we retrieve information and connect it to new experiences, the stronger our understanding becomes around that topic and idea.

Which is why most of you reading this chapter have a better sense of how to drive a car than how photosynthesis works. Even though photosynthesis happens every day all around you, it does not impact you, or in other words, it does not grab your attention. Driving a car, on the other hand, is connected to your daily life as an adult for work, pleasure, and all other kinds of reasons.

Our students, just like all of us, tend to prioritize the learning of things that will impact them. It is in our nature to pay attention (and kick off the learning process) with information that is connected to our interests and needs.

School Reimagined

Remember all those words that were put in front of *learning* mentioned at the beginning of this chapter? **They are important because teachers and educators are realizing that school has not been personalized, individualized, or blended for a long time.**

For years *school* was focused on common experiences, compliance in policies and procedures, standard assessments, and gradual release of information to the masses.

Learning has never been like that. We've always binged learned topics we are interested about, assessed ourselves in what we did with that knowledge, and changed the procedures for learning depending on the circumstance and environment.

Nothing about learning has ever been standard.

Blended learning used to be between learning by listening and learning by reading. Now it is often used to talk about learning online and learning in-person.

Personalized learning used to be going to a library and picking out the books you were interested in reading and learning more about. Today, personalized learning is working through playlists of content and information and tailored activities.

The shift we are seeing in schools, classrooms, and learning environments around the world right now is a renewed focus on learning, and less of a focus on school.

That's a big change for a lot of educators who were brought up in this school environment, taught in this school environment, and prepared to teach in this school environment.

But if you are struggling or know someone struggling with the shift back to learning, remind yourself that we've always learned in personalized, individualized, and blended ways. It's time to embrace the notion that school should be a lot more focused on learning quality and a lot less focused on a common learning experience.

Project-based learning provides the perfect forum to allow for these choices and roadmaps to converge in an authentic way (both in and out of school). It is not on the outside of personalized or individualized learning, instead think of it as a way to make learning feel natural again.

Go to THEPBLPLAYBOOK.com for more resources, materials, and guiding questions about this chapter.

CHAPTER 17:

Creating Your PBL from Scratch (a Checklist)

XOXXOXOOXO

Three of my favorite project-based learning experiences took shape in completely different ways and circumstances.

My students and I created **"Project: Global Inform"** together, after tweaking the original assignment. My students were studying genocide and human rights violations, and the culminating activity was writing a letter/e-mail to a politician who could help stop the injustices that were happening around the world, or in our own community. My students wanted to do more, and Project: Global Inform was born. Instead of writing letters, their groups created Awareness Campaigns using multimedia, social media, and good ol' word of mouth to push the conversation much wider and farther than a single letter would do.

My students loved the **Flat Classroom Project**. This was created by Vicki Davis and Julie Lindsay. We jumped in full-steam collaborating with students from four different countries to research topics like outsourcing, future of work, off-shoring, insourcing, supply chaining, and more. Then they created videos to share their collaborative research and analysis. This project was a dive into global PBL, and we were both challenged by the content, but also by the time difference and cultural differences that came working with students from around the globe.

The **20% Project** (a.k.a. Genius Hour) was a third project that actually started from complete scratch. We jumped in without a true roadmap as students came up with a purpose, passion, and strategy for what they would learn and create over the semester. With many ups and downs, came a lot of wins and losses. But above all else, the students were engaged, empowered, and also a bit uneasy with the process. We shared our failed attempts widely throughout the project, and the final presentations were live-streamed to an authentic audience.

In each case (Project: Global Inform, Flat Classroom Project, 20% Project), the PBL transformed not only how my students were learning but also how they were assessed on their learning and could demonstrate their understanding. All three of these projects not only were successful but also were tweaked in subsequent years with other classes. None of them were a "finished product" in the sense that there was no room for growth. There was a ton of learning that happened on my end!

Why is this so important?

Well, I get the question all the time: **Where do I start with PBL?**

The answer I give here has three parts because I believe you can start in three separate areas on your project-based learning journey.

#1. Start with a proven project that you can adopt and adapt as you see fit with your students.

This happened when we did the Flat Classroom Project. This was created by Vicki Davis and Julie Lindsay. They crafted the project with each other, building on the work they were each doing with students and focused on the premise of having a global learning project where students from around the world could collaborate with each other.

They were the chefs of this project, and I was a cook, taking notes on the recipe along the way. They provided goals, outcomes, a step-by-step process, meetings to coordinate, deadlines, and assessments for the student work.

As the teacher, there were certain areas of the project I had to tweak and change along the way. This was giving my students more time to research, and more time to create their videos. It was connecting with other teachers in the project to make sure our students were connecting and collaborating online. It was stepping in for a teachable moment about playing games with your new friends from Europe versus working together.

Yet the project design allowed me to have much more freedom as a guide because I was not worried the entire time about whether things would work and how students would engage with the content. This had all been predesigned and planned by Vicki, Julie, and their team.

Starting with a proven template gave me the boost I needed to try out different types of PBL with my students after a successful experience.

#2. Modify an existing activity, assessment, unit, or project.

We had recently read *Night* by Elie Wiesel, and this quote in particular guided our campaign to create awareness about human rights violations:

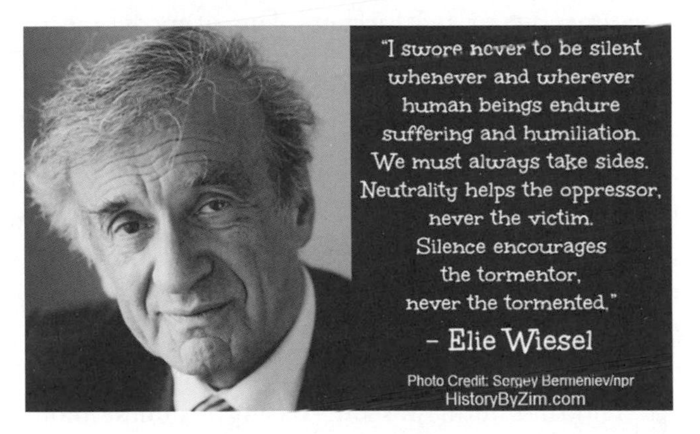

After our discussion about human rights violations, child soldiers, and genocide that was currently happening in our world right now—my students wanted to DO something.

As a class, we decided to not be bystanders and to take a side. This new project would be a chance to use our voice to spread awareness.

Traditionally, during this unit, students had written a position paper on the Holocaust and genocide in general, as well as send a letter/e-mail to a senator about a current human rights violation.

My group of students wanted to take this further. Together we crafted a new project that would focus on creating awareness about current human rights violations.

I say WE because the students had a lot of input into how this project would look, what they would be measured on, and what the ultimate goals and objectives would be.

Project: Global Inform (PGI) was created in the 2008–2009 school year. The students picked their own groups and researched current human rights violations. Each group picked a violation they felt particularly passionate about and began to develop an action plan. Their action plans allowed the students to judge how effective each method of media was at spreading information and creating awareness.

At the end of Project: Global Inform's first run, hundreds of people had been met face-to-face with information they did not know, while thousands of other teens and young adults saw videos, visited websites, and became Twitter and Facebook fans of media meant to create awareness.

In 2009–2010, Wissahickon High School took Project: Global Inform to the next level. Over 110 students participated, and this time the students were even more creative. In addition to the video, web, and Facebook campaigns, groups began to host events dedicated to raising awareness for their cause. This time, not only was information spread, but money was also raised for organizations currently fighting against human rights violations. Thousands of dollars were raised in just under six weeks, showing that students do have the power to make a difference.

Project: Global Inform was one of my proudest moments as a teacher. It still gives me chills when I look at the work these sixteen- and seventeen-year-old students were doing to spread awareness on such serious violations.

And it was part of our curriculum, not an added piece. Layer the work into curriculum instead of making it something added to the work you are already doing.

This was a case of modifying something existing into something that created a better learning experience through PBL.

#3. Planning a PBL Unit from Scratch

Katherine von Jan explains how Google's idea came to be in her article, "Pursue Passion: Demand Google 20% Time at School":

Google's "20% Time," inspired by Sergey Brin's and Larry Page's Montessori School experience, is a philosophy and policy that every Google employee spend 20% of their time (the equivalent of a full work day each week) working on ideas and projects that interest that employee. They are encouraged to explore anything other than their normal day-to-day job. As a result, 50% of all Google's products by 2009 originated from the 20% free time, including Gmail. Real break-through happens when we are free from others' expectations and driven by individual passion.[31]

When I read her article and finished Dan Pink's book *Drive,* I had to seriously reconsider what I was doing with my students. Extrinsic motivation can only go so far in education, and above everything else I want my students to be people who enjoy learning. However, as educators many times we are constrained by curriculum and standards. This idea came and went during the fall months before resurfacing in December 2011.

In December, two things happened that made me decide almost immediately that this had to happen. First, I was part of the curriculum process at my school and really started to delve into the "why we do what we do" questions that alluded me most of the time during the daily grind. I also was reading texts about "inquiry-based learning" and the "understanding by design" framework.

Second, I was challenged by Thomas Gaffey (he's the best math teacher I've ever met) to do "new things in new ways" at the Microsoft Innovative Educator program. The 20% Time seemed like a new way to engage and motivate students to learn. If we want to prepare students in high school to be lifelong learners, assets to their communities, and able to take a successful next step in their academic lives (i.e., college), then this project would change not only my pedagogy, but also their view on learning after high school.

The day after winter break I "assigned the project." In essence, high school students have spent most of their academic lives being told what to do. Their grades are then dependent on how well they completed the assigned tasks. Most teenagers spend their free time doing things they are "not told to do." For example, most parents aren't yelling at their son to play video games, or at their daughter to spend three hours on Facebook. These actions are done because teenagers want to do them (and in part because they are told many times not to do this). My class agreed that most teenagers "want to do what they want to do, and not what others tell them."

So this project, I said, was me telling them to do something that they want to do, with their time that it is usually spent doing what other people want them to do (that's a mouthful). The guidelines were simple. Here is the handout:

The 20% Project

1. For the rest of the year, 20% of your time in my class will be spent creating something you want to make.
2. It has to be some type of learning, and you have to document it (journal, etc.).
3. You'll present your accomplishments to the class twice (and will not be graded on it).
4. That's it. Have fun. Find your passion. Explore it. Enjoy learning what you want.

X____

Mass confusion set in. Most of my students were trying to figure out what the catch was, asking questions like: "So what are we getting credit for?" "What kinds of things can we do?" "Why aren't we being graded?" and "I don't get it, Mr. J, what are we supposed to be doing?"

After a few more minutes of explanation, my students began to come around. I was not going to grade them on this project, but I was going to keep them accountable. Many times in education, we believe the only way to hold students accountable is by giving some form of assessment. For this project, they began documenting their learning through writing (also, possible podcasts or video journals), and they presented to the class their "learning journey" through a TED-style talk.

After creating this project from scratch, it got me thinking about the best practices around project-based learning.

How do we identify proven (preexisting) PBL experiences that will work for our students?

How do we tweak and modify existing activities and units to a PBL experience that will work for our learners?

How do we create a PBL unit from scratch, while hitting the key pieces that make up effective PBL?

The following is a checklist we've been using to plan, create, modify, and assess various PBL units and experiences. It is by no means a complete unit-planning guide, but instead, a one-page checklist that identifies the key areas of effective PBL and forces you to consider whether the project you are doing with your students has many of these pieces involved.

Because many teachers, schools, and districts already have lesson planning guidelines and best practices around how they create units, we needed to create something flexible.

This checklist can work with any preexisting PBL unit as an auditing tool. It can work while you are modifying an activity into a PBL experience as a place to start. And, for those of you creating a PBL unit from scratch, it can be a guiding document to start the process and check where your project stands.

A Checklist for Planning a PBL Unit

GOALS/OUTCOME

____ **Teacher**-defined learning goals
____ **Learner**-defined learning goals

Note: There were many successful PBL experiences where I (as the teacher) defined all the learning goals. However, when my students had some voice in their learning goals and outcomes, the engagement rose right from the beginning. Depending on age level and circumstances, you may check only one of these boxes.

Skills

____ **Core** standards specific to level/subject
____ **Cognitive** skills
____ **Soft** skills (or twenty-first-century skills)
____ **ISTE NETS** skills

Note: There are many different skills and standards that can be acquired, mastered, and assessed during PBL. The key here is to identify these before, during, and after the PBL experience.

Experience

____ **Problem/question** is defined at the start of the project.
____ **Problem/question** is refined during the project.
____ **Authentic Audience** is defined before the start of the project.
____ **Authentic Audience** is refined during the project.

Note: I keep problem/question combined here, but sometimes it may be both, or they may be separate. PBL (especially if you are looking at it through the lens of the design process) may also start with a product in mind, awareness of an issue, a natural phenomenon, or empathy. In each of these cases, they'll have a guiding question and/or problem that pushes the work forward. An audience is a key component because it makes the problem/question relevant to the learner in an authentic way (instead of just playing the game of school).

Learning

____ **Learning targets** are defined and measurable.

____ **Standards** are aligned to tasks throughout the experience.

____ **Student choice** in any of following: content, process, tools, materials, technology, and demonstrating understanding.

Note: Learning is the goal of PBL. Student choice drives ownership, which drives engagement/empowerment, and ultimately a deeper learning experience. Understanding how the standards and learning targets are connected to the PBL process is part of the planning that moves a project past just being an arts and crafts activity.

Collaboration

____ **Learners** collaborate with each other.

____ **Work** with mentors.

Note: Collaboration can take shape in many different forms. Even if the PBL experience is an individual process, collaboration is an authentic piece of the research and working with mentors levels up the relevancy of the work.

PRODUCT

____ **Time** built in for reflection and an iterative process.

____ **Product** is created and made available to a real audience.

Note: A product does not have to be a physical product. It can be a digital product. It can be an experience. It can be a movement. It can be an event. There are many different creative forms of a product, so be sure to not limit what this might look like. Providing time and support for reflection, self-assessment, and iteration is a key to making something worthy of sharing with a real audience that can benefit from the product.

Go to THEPBLPLAYBOOK.com for more resources, materials, and guiding questions about this chapter.

CHAPTER 18:

The Whole Course PBL Experience

XOXXOXOOXO

The previous chapters showed how Project-Based Learning has worked its way into all kinds of grade levels and subject areas. It can be just as effective with six-year-olds as it is with high school seniors. Yet, in many cases, PBL has grown well beyond a part of the classroom experience to being an entire course or school experience.

The following stories are examples of PBL happening across the curriculum in multiple disciplines as an entire course or program. You'll hear from real teachers and school leaders who are doing this work, as they'll share the ups and downs of making PBL a whole course experience.

Anne Krolicki

Princeville Jr./Sr. High School, English and Mass Communications teacher, Co-teach interdisciplinary English III/ US History

4 years of teaching experience

The American Experience

The course description for Anne Krolicki and her coteacher Chris Bergschneider's PBL project states that students will explore American history through both literary and informative texts. Rather than focusing on specific events or people, students will explore the American experience through topics and movements, tracking the development of a nation and its people. This interdisciplinary course will build and strengthen students' individual reading and writing skills while simultaneously enhancing their understanding of America's past and students' role in its future.

The teaching team addresses a wide variety of the Illinois social studies standards as well as their 11–12 Common Core ELA standards. They also incorporate ISTE standards into instruction. Using the Marzano (2017) approach to competencies, they have combined standards to create more cohesive checkpoints for kids to measure their movement toward and beyond proficiency.

Anne and Chris have both used PBL in their separate classrooms before, but certainly not as an entire course, and certainly not to this extent where students get to work on different standards at different times depending on what they find important within the topic of study. They had never heard of anyone using PBL quite this way, but when they decided to teach this class together, they started with what their ideal would be (within the confines of the school schedule, that is), and then tried to create it. This is what they came up with. They've had two units where kids design the projects, and three where they've given them a few more parameters because they weren't used to the design process yet having come from an incredibly traditional environment before (workbooks, hour-long grammar lectures, etc.). They needed to ease them into projects first and then design.

Students learn content at an individualized pace through video lessons, whole group, small group, and one-on-one instruction and design projects by developing research questions and writing project proposals. After receiving feedback multiple times from instructors through teacher-designed checkpoints and conferencing, students revise and share their final products with classroom and authentic audiences. While all students write informative, persuasive, and narrative writing throughout the year, they choose the writing style they feel best suits their current topic of study and their particular research questions within that study. Many students have expressed that they see themselves as writers for the first time because they are creating content shared with and useful for others, and they receive immediate, face-to-face feedback on their individual strengths and weaknesses.

The biggest difference is in who these kids are now. Kids are coming in during homeroom, before and after school, and they're constantly e-mailing questions and asking for advice, not to hit a point on the rubric, but because they are genuinely just more motivated and interested. Anne, Chris, and their students all struggled at the beginning of the year because it was so new, and honestly, the kids weren't loving it at first. It was much harder than they thought it would be, and that's not to say that everyone loves it now. Some kids want to go back to the worksheets and lectures because, while boring, they were good at that game. But those same students talk about how they are writers now. It's such a powerful thing for Anne and Chris to hear them call themselves writers when they didn't before. They say they know how to research and understand that it's not about finding facts, but about how you analyze and do something with that information. They are talking about race and gender issues. They are becoming people who are ready to navigate a complex world with complex problems. Anne knows that's not an outcome easily measured, but it's the one for which she is most proud of them.

Anne explains that she and Chris design four checkpoints for each unit. Students assess themselves during each of the four conferences and show evidence while they lead the conversation. These first two checkpoints are about developing the research questions and the written project proposal. This lets all parties know how strong the project design is. They give their feedback and then make a decision together about where they are in progress. The same is true for checkpoint three, but this "rubric" looks exactly the same as their fourth checkpoint (depending on which writing style/type they are using). This is their "in-progress" project check so that they know which areas they need to focus most in during revision. Then they present their projects on the last day of the unit, and Anne and Chris complete checkpoint four as the "summative" for the project.

Of course, Anne admits, they've had both epic success and epic failure from students. Notably one of the toughest failures was in their first unit, which was their history of education unit, when a student (we'll call him Patrick) turned in the answers to his essential questions without actually submitting a project. He had a plan that was approved in his second checkpoint, and in his third checkpoint, he had done all his research and answered his question but hadn't started putting all of it together into an informed action item that could be shared and stir change. When they asked him why he hadn't created a project, he didn't have an answer. In further conversations, Anne came to realize that several of their students had never had this kind of freedom before. They had a lot of great ideas to make projects, but even with the checkpoints and feedback, many of them felt helpless to troubleshoot and problem-solve. It was a big eye-opener for Anne and Chris as teachers. They truly felt that giving kids the freedom they'd been begging for—to explore their interests within a topic and create something of their own—would unlock their potential and bring incredible outcomes, and while it did for many of their kids, a good amount felt overwhelmed by applying their learning and developing critical thinking and design skills. After that first unit, they took a step away from the more personalized, inquiry-based PBL and into three units of more "product-driven" (as John Spencer has called this type of PBL).

In their criminal justice unit, students explored high-profile cases in history, explained their significance, created a script, and performed it in front of their classmates who acted as the jury. In their economics unit, students all became marketing consultants and chose an American company to investigate. They had to develop a multistrategy proposal based on finances, marketing, advertising, product lines, etc. and then "pitch" to the board of the company, showing they understood the history of the company in order to make quality suggestions about the future of it. Doing these more explicit projects helped the kids get a better grasp on the idea of PBL and what it required of them. Then, Anne and Chris were able to give more freedom again and ease them back into designing their own projects within the theme of the unit.

Patrick's struggles supplied a learning opportunity for Anne and Chris which likely helped multiple other students ease into the PBL way of learning by helping their educators realize how to better facilitate each and every student. There was also one very big win for this teaching duo after introducing their PBL project. When two parents came in for conferences, they were in tears because they felt that their children had, in the past, been overlooked because they weren't "typically successful" students. In Anne's class, they were able to be part of the conversation and could explore an interest with parameters, which made them want to work harder and see value in a subject which had always made them feel less-than. In their quest for answers to their research questions, students have made contact with major corporations and universities, and created products that have the ability to change our community. One student is writing a children's book series, and any money that she makes will fund another student's community-problem-solving project. These two girls are in the process of setting up a nonprofit organization and have made some incredible contacts to help them accomplish their goals. It has been so rewarding for Anne to have kids pass her in the hallway in the morning and already be asking where the conference/feedback sign-up list is for each of them. They are excited for feedback, and they are applying it because they are getting that critical feedback when it matters—multiple times throughout the unit.

Anne admits that it is incredibly hard to organize the projects sometimes, but she thinks that's important, too. The kids have seen her struggle, and that's so powerful for them—to know that she's not just preaching challenges to them, but that she's living it right alongside of them. Anne also explains that some of their parents struggled even more. They faced some harsh criticism in the community from some parents who just didn't understand and refused to come in to discuss matters with them. Anne has always had great relationships with her students' parents, and for the first time, she was struggling to feel like she could even reach them. Anne and Chris overcame that by continuing to adapt for and have conversations with their kids. Those conversations have been the key because once the kids buy-in, the parents usually do, too. While their students don't take any traditional tests throughout the year for her class, on their winter standardized progress monitor, Anne's students saw *incredible* growth—more than she's seen from her class and at that grade level in a long time.

On top of that, Anne can't stress enough how important administrative support is to learning/skill-building outcomes for kids. She believes that sometimes people see the teacher as the main influence for kids, and while obviously there is a lot of truth in that, none of this would be happening if Anne's principal, and her superintendent, didn't share ideas and encourage their teachers to try new things and push kids to develop the skills they need to become lifelong, independent learners.

Having that collaborative team has been so important to Anne's growth as a teacher. She knows that when she gets better, she does better for her students. She jumped in because her mentors and leaders jumped in with her. She has never felt alone or unsupported, which has made it easier to try.

Once you teach this way, it's awfully difficult to see a lot of value in many of the traditional ways of assessing students. Using PBL means Anne gets to see all the learning. She is able to watch it and guide it and feel their frustration and celebrate their success. She sees the figurative wheels turning and knows exactly where each kid is in terms of skills. She is confident that it means her kids are more prepared for life.

Jennifer Solt

Thompson Valley High School, Loveland, CO; classroom teacher
12+ years of teaching experience
Opening the Locked Door: Mystery, Curiosity, Design Thinking, and the Escape Room

From the course handbook Jennifer Solt has written for her students: The Challenge: Using the design-thinking process, how can we use our passions, interests, and skills as a team to create and pitch a high-quality escape room design that challenges players to think critically, have fun, and work together?

This semester project is designed to stretch your abilities and to encourage you to think critically, to solve a challenging problem, and to demonstrate your abilities in research, planning and implementation, teamwork, writing, organization, persuasion, and public speaking. Your project will, by nature, be interdisciplinary—requiring you to apply skills or investigate issues across many different subject areas and integrating and showcasing the knowledge and skills you've acquired over the past 12+ years in school. The project is intended to bridge the transition away from teacher-centric and subject-specific learning to a real-life experience relevant to the next stage of your life that is more closely aligned to collegiate studies and career environments.

The final pitches are made to a community team of escape room business owners in Northern Colorado. Because the PBL is semester-long, we work through all of the Common Core ELA standards for grade 12.

When Jennifer was asked to take over the course, she asked the administrators if she could try a capstone-style PBL model for the course. For four semesters, this one-semester course was "The Power of One," and students designed a project that defined and solved a problem in the world. We had students who raised hundreds to thousands of dollars for local organizations like The House of Neighborly Service, the Humane Society, and Make a Wish Foundation through fundraising events they held. Other students designed products: a backpack for diabetics to keep both school supplies and diabetic supplies, an ankle brace that ties directly into a football cleat to better support a healing ankle, a water purifier for backpackers and hunters, cattle fencing that eliminates injury to livestock. Some students created call-to-action campaigns: a club for new students to get acquainted to their school community, an antibullying campaign, and lessons in rape culture and a shift in mind-set. Some students looked into the development of local spaces: a new bike park on old Hewlett Packard land and changes to the safety conditions of our district-owned baseball field. All students were challenged to reach beyond the walls of the classroom in the implementation of their ideas.

Jennifer's pass rate has greatly increased and her students are far more engaged in the course (spring semester seniors are notoriously difficult to keep engaged through graduation, but the originality of their projects and the personalization the course design has afforded has helped immensely). Administrators from across the district (and from other districts) are often brought to Jennifer's classroom to observe the work of her students. This year, in an attempt at more team collaboration and to try a different iteration (Jennifer is a designer, too, after all) of the course, Jennifer decided to try out an escape room design focus.

Jennifer introduces the design challenge to them, practices with mini-design challenges early in the semester, and then begin going through the steps of the design-challenge, beginning with exploring what an escape room is, asking a lot of questions, and analyzing mystery-genre texts (print and movie). They write their own narrative as a mystery short story. They do a lot of exploration of their interests and talents and then they write and record "elevator pitches" for themselves (Jennifer uses the Flipgrid app for this) and talk a little bit about the narrative they designed. They watch each other's presentations, taking notes about their classmates. Then, Jennifer holds a "hiring fair" for them to form teams. They interview each other and figure out the best combination of team members. They decide which narrative they want to use as the foundation for their escape room (or decide to make a hybrid of several of them). Then, they begin throwing new questions out to each other to figure out what they need to do to win the escape room competition and to have a high-quality design and pitch. They each write a proposal letter for what they're planning to do and who is responsible for what in the research stage (Jennifer guides them in how to write business letters, and they use this format for the proposal). This helps her know how to support them as they move forward and ensures each member of the team is working toward the same idea—Jennifer has been able to catch some miscommunication in the early stages by doing this.

They then move into the research portion of the class. They divide up research tasks and begin exploring through the Internet, visiting escape rooms, contacting local business owners, comparison shopping for supplies, trying out designs, etc. Jennifer has learned that this works best if they go back and forth between ideation and research until they feel, as a team, they have enough to begin a prototype (initially, ideation was not begun until research was complete, but Jennifer learned that these stages need to be very fluid). For the English standards of the course, they keep detailed research notes that they turn in, they each write an abstract of their findings (in place of the traditional lengthy research paper), and they create MLA bibliographies of their research. Additionally, at the end of ideation, teams have a detailed project concept map and a functional narrative on which the room is built.

The next stage is prototyping. During this stage, Jennifer and her students talk a lot about audience and each team identifies someone within their target audience to serve as a tester of their prototype. They are also responsible for drafting their room's budget during this stage. The completion of this stage includes turning in their tester's notes, a budget, and their prototype. Their work often leads back to earlier stages before they feel ready to turn these pieces in and to move to the next stage.

The "final" stage of launching their idea requires a five-minute professional pitch video creation that includes logos, ethos, and pathos. These videos go to our community members for feedback and rankings for the competition portion (Jennifer buys the winning team entry tickets to a local escape room). Again, this stage sometimes means going back to an earlier stage for perfecting and resubmitting, as teams have time.

Students forget they are in a language arts class. They are combining math, science, art, language, and so much more, depending on the designs they plan. Some students delve deep into historical documents to learn about a particular time period in which their room is set, or about particular personalities from the past who are characters in their room's narratives. Some students do detailed geometric calculations to figure out how to construct a portion of their room. The budgets they create have moved them into questions about the minimum wage and salary work, about the cost of rental space within the community, and about purchasing second-hand materials and materials that need less maintenance. Beautiful logos, murals, and costumes have appeared in the prototypes. Students with skills in video productions create interesting entry-videos for participants, and students who love the hands-on work of their construction and welding classes are finding a niche for their skills on a team as three-dimensional portions of the project come together.

Students that are normally okay with a "D" on an assignment are going back to their work over and over again to improve it because it matters to the end design. The professional pitch means more to them than a presentation to their classmates. From Jennifer's perspective, the most important change has been that she has become a facilitator. She has time to work with students one-on-one, to really get to know them and what they're doing after high school, and to help them grow from where they are instead of teaching to the middle and hoping the high-flyers find something to challenge themselves and the low-ability students can keep up. Every time Jennifer attends an IEP meeting for someone in this class, the parents express amazement at how much their child is achieving and Jennifer knows she's meeting the demands of the IEP because she's working with kids individually—and they're working with each other: challenging each other, helping each other, providing feedback, finding unique ways to remove barriers.

There are still students who would rather take a traditional, literature-based English course. Jennifer understands that this doesn't appeal to every single student, but she has a lot of course options for students with that interest. She tends to have the students who have never liked English class and have traditionally given up early in the semester or settled for a low grade. These are the students who amaze themselves. Two of Jennifer's seniors this fall were students who seldom came to school when she knew them as freshmen. They never missed a day of her senior class, they put their hearts into their projects, and they shared how proud they were of their room and their perseverance.

Jennifer has her students finish the course with a reflection on the semester. Without fail, the vast majority of them comment that the element of the course they found most challenging was also the part they felt was most important to what comes next for them after graduation: time management. Most of them have never had the choice to figure out for themselves how to get from point A to point B over the course of a whole semester. Jennifer gives a lot of support and check-ins, but they manage this. When the first week of research shows a lot of kids on their phones or in conversation unrelated to the project, Jennifer lets it happen. She reminds them of the impact of this, but she lets it happen. Then they talk about this as they begin to catch the excitement of the project and to see how time matters. It's a tough lesson for some of them, but this is almost always what the seniors talk about in their reflection. "I learned I waste a lot of time and can get very distracted. I was fired from my team. That was hard, but when I was hired by a different team I knew I couldn't blow it again. Every minute counts. I used my time well, I put my phone away—that was hard—but I did it. Our room is so cool! I can't wait to get results from the escape room owners."

An exciting piece of information Jennifer likes to share is that she got rid of her teacher desk this year. She's never sitting in it anymore, and she needs the space to spread student spaces out and to be able to move around their workspaces to check in while they work. Jennifer believes the room should be about them and not be a monument of her workspace. There is now a sofa in her room and some flexible workspaces. There are no longer rows of student desks but, instead, pods of four that get moved throughout the day to accommodate different types of groupings.

Jennifer is also proud to be much more connected with her larger community. Her students have needed help contacting city council members, school board members, business leaders, etc., through the years of using PBL. There is a real audience who is so much more powerful than a letter grade she can give. Jennifer had to dig deep to find contacts and to talk regularly to people in the community about what they're trying to accomplish and how they can help. The awesome flip side of this is that her community is getting to know her kids—not the ones spray-painting the side of their building or the one yelling an obscenity out of a car window, but the one donating money to the homeless shelter, the one holding a 5K walk to raise money for abused animals, and the one changing the world for the better.

One of Jennifer's students a few years ago had been involved in an armed robbery just months before she had him. During English 12, he and his partner identified the problem of pedestrian accidents in intersections and sought a solution. They had an idea for pylons that came out of the pavement when the traffic light changed, but, because the course requirement is to reach out of the classroom with their ideas she pushed them in their research and they began e-mailing one of the city traffic engineers to ask about traffic patterns, accident rates, and the feasibility of their idea. Jennifer was amazed at the energy and empathy for others that this student poured into this project. He was amazed that people in city offices cared about a high school kid enough to take his ideas seriously and e-mail him back. The self-efficacy he gained from this interaction cannot be understated.

One of the hardest transitions for Jennifer was learning how to build "classroom culture" in PBL. She realizes that when you're standing in front of the room, asking questions, hearing the "whole class" share, there are common situations and ideas that create humor and collective awareness around certain causes. The inside jokes and the shared concerns that come up build a classroom dynamic and develop relationship.

When the students are working on their own ideas at their own pace and you blend in among them as they work, any commonality of a class seems to disappear. Building relationships looks different. Jennifer struggled with this more than anything else. Her advice is to be patient. She knows her students so much better because she's sitting with them one-on-one and helping them work through the questions.

PBL-teaching is still a relatively new idea in Jennifer's district, so her students come expecting to be spoon-fed information in the traditional assembly-line version of education everyone is used to. There is an early level of frustration that comes when she asks them to ask (and answer) the questions. When she and her class read a text, they come up with the discussion points. When they work on a project, they generate ideas and identify the problems in their work. This takes infinitely more brainpower than being told what a metaphor is or that a character change is imminent in this passage and have them identify and share it back. During her first semester of using the PBL model, one student said, "Can't you just give us a test? I'd much rather answer multiple choice questions than have to do all of this work." Again, be patient. The students get a lot out of this and can see it in the end, but it takes time to get comfortable with PBL for them and for the instructor. Also, mini-projects help the kids see the design process over a class period or a week and how it empowers them to do their best thinking before they jump into the big project. Jennifer attests that she is an all-in kind of person, but many of her students need a taste of it before they buy in, and that's understandable.

Amy Foley on behalf of the Innovation Institute, Shanghai American School, China

Current Innovation Institute team:

Year 1 (grade 9)—Patrice Parks (English), James Linzel (Physics/Chemistry), Dave Wood (History), Kim Sajan (Creativity and Design)

Year 2 (grade 10)—Tiffany Kelley (English), JuLain Mooney (Biology), Tom Musk (Social Studies—AP Seminar), David Gran (Innovation and Design), Innovation Institute Coordinator (and previous teacher)—Amy Foley

The Innovation Institute program originated from a series of conversations between high school faculty and administration. Several teachers were inspired by their previous educational and professional experiences. After numerous discussions (at least one of which was based upon Jared Diamond's *Guns, Germs, and Steel*), James Linzel and Tom Musk spoke with their high school principal at the time, Sascha Heckmann. They were inspired to help develop a program driven by phenomena or issues-based perspectives. These conversations began to include more teachers as they gained momentum and became more structured as they focused on subject integration and overlap. Eventually, the program was approved, school administration secured financial support, and professional learning opportunities were provided for teachers (including time to collaborate on program development).

Conversations around meaningful outcomes and pedagogical philosophies, as well as developing deeper understandings of each other's content areas, were important steps in creating the Innovation Institute program and specific interdisciplinary projects, recalls Patrice Parks. She explains that it took about six months to address both philosophical and practical aspects of the program. Understanding collectively what project or problem-based learning was going to look like in their particular context—a private, college prep school in Asia—was essential to creating a program that honored their responsibility to their students, to parents' expectations of an SAS education, and to their belief in what education can and should achieve.

Tom explains that teachers found it to be an incredibly challenging process to get the program started, and it felt high-stakes at the time because the school invested so much money into infrastructure. He feels that this program would not have survived, and ultimately thrived, without administrative support and teachers willing to support and inspire one another. In addition, Patrice says that pioneering students who were willing to take a leap of faith in a tradition-bound educational environment were also instrumental.

Another challenge, according to Patrice, is that it is deeply difficult to de-program/wean (for lack of a better term) students from the traditional classroom educational paradigm, but it can be done. The fact that this is a two-year program is essential to its success because it takes real time and effort to shift students' horizons of expectations around their learning experiences. The first year (grade 9) lays down the fundamentals in skills and content for the disciplines, as well as the 5 C's (Collaboration, Creativity, Communication, Critical Thinking, and Compassion). The second year (grade 10) enables students to continue the journey and takes them to the next level of conceptual understanding and a better grasp of the 5 C's.

Ultimately, all of the conversations, planning days and professional development led to the creation of a two-year, interdisciplinary, PBL program where students are expected to attempt to answer four to six "driving questions" per year using their learning from Design, English, History, and Science. James explains that these questions are focused on contemporary challenges such as: "How to endure justly on a finite world," "What is the biggest catalyst for change in China?," or "How do we adapt to scarcity in a globalized world?" David Gran points out that in the Institute, content is not emphasized over skills. Instead, students start with real-world applications and meaningful integrations and work backwards from there.

Amy further explains that the driving questions (DQs) are always open-ended and can be answered in a variety of ways. In addition, student teams must draw upon their knowledge from all four disciplines to fully address the DQ. Depending on the project, students are involved in foundational learning prior to, or just after, the project launch. This foundational learning often involves students attending separate classes for each discipline as they would in a more traditional program. However, teachers co-plan in advance to ensure that what is being taught connects to the other classes and is also setting students up to be able to later further their understanding in order to answer the DQ.

After each project launch, the teachers' role is to facilitate the process each team goes through to incubate their potential answers for the DQ. Team contracts are written, and teams are given time to ideate (brainstorm). Patrice says that while it can be difficult, teams must be given time to pursue less than stellar ideas far enough that they either realize on their own that their idea is going nowhere or is not deep enough to adequately answer the question. At times, student teams need to be redirected by a teacher facilitator. This can be tricky as there is usually only

6–7 weeks allocated for each project. When designs/products/research have to be cast aside, both students and teachers begin to feel the pressure. Timing for teacher intervention is important—and delicate.

In fact, helping students to collaborate effectively is one of the main challenges throughout the program. Students need help learning what collaboration looks like and feels like. To go beyond cooperative work to true collaboration, honesty and vulnerability is required. Patrice further explains that PBL can go the way of polite divisions of labor that prevent inspiration, depth, or innovation—or can perhaps lead to one responsible and driven student doing most, if not all, of the work. One way to avoid this is for teachers to model true collaboration. Patrice and other Institute teachers often share some of their challenges in becoming a truly collaborative team. The teachers also often hold meetings in spaces where students can observe teachers' processes and how they negotiate conflict and honor each other. Teachers ensure that students know how to reach out for help when then need a mediator to help the team get back on track. Institute teachers also model hypothetical situations and frequently conference with student teams.

An exciting element of collaboration for students is the big reveal of teams during a project launch. Teachers may solicit input from students when forming teams for a new project, but ultimately teachers finalize teams that they feel are balanced and best accommodate students' needs. However, it is a puzzle trying to ensure all teams will be successful. One interdisciplinary project requires grade-10 students to design and build a board game to answer the question "How do we adapt to scarcity in a globalized world?" Tom recalls that during this project, there was a team that teachers were concerned about. The students were solid individually, but there was uncertainty about how they would work together, as well as whether any would step up as a leader. As the ideation process unfolded, the team really struggled to find a unifying idea to answer the driving question. However, in the final few weeks of the project—when other teams were iterating their final product based upon the expert feedback from a game consultant—one student made a joke about creating a game about competitive sushi chefs who compete to destroy each other. After further discussion and brainstorming, the group decided it was actually a good idea that would allow them to answer the DQ.

Ultimately, the team produced an exemplary game that truly impressed parents and visitors during the Family Game Night showcase. Tom points out that this is a great example that team strength is not simply assembling strong individuals—it is about groups collaborating effectively. As an end note to this story, for the final project of the two-year program (eight months later), student managers were given the freedom to assemble their own teams. Perhaps not surprisingly, these four students chose to be a team again because they knew they could persevere and work well together. They ended up producing another fantastic project.

Another key element of the program is incorporating experts or members of the community. Tiffany Kelley explains that Institute teachers want to empower students to see the world as their classroom, and the meaningful connections students make with experts, authentic audiences, and even places visited outside of school during PBL, contributes deeply to their engagement in the learning process and ultimately to their final products. It can be challenging to secure experts, so at times teachers have asked parents, other faculty, or members of the communications department to act as experts or audiences. Tiffany has observed that sometimes these experts are giving the same message as the Institute teachers, but having another voice say something in a different way to the students can have a profound effect.

Authentic products or audiences are also a focus for the Innovation Institute. Grade-10 students complete a film project to answer the driving question "Do we live in a Brave New World?" Both years that students submitted films to the Shanghai Student Film Festival, teams won awards. David explains that the significance of this is that Institute students were competing against more experienced film students, while this was the first film the Institute students had produced. Innovation Institute students most likely created impressive films because they were exceptionally skilled at working together as a collaborative team in their undertaking of creative tasks. The technical skill of film can be challenging, but effective collaboration is crucial for most fledgling film crews.

Finally, time must be made for reflection. Student teams need to be guided through a reflection of how well their team worked together, and students need to individually reflect on how they could better support their team in the future. Student feedback can also be useful to help teachers refine projects and PBL structures. Institute teachers often seek student feedback before launching a newly-designed project. Running a protocol with a small group of students gives them input into the project and helps teachers to improve the project prior to an official launch. Amy recommends that teacher teams set aside time—both during and after a project—to regularly reflect and document necessary improvements. Teacher reflection helps to improve the program. For example, David recognizes that Institute teachers have learned over time to more effectively incorporate individual accountability through specific roles, teacher check-ins, and student peer reviews both during and at the end of projects.

It is really important for teachers to remember that taking risks or implementing something innovative is sometimes overwhelming, says Amy. There are many obstacles along the way. However, focus on positives such as students who are benefitting from the program. The following quote is from a student who spoke about their experience after they had completed the two-year Innovation Institute program.

> *In Inno, every major project we had was a ride of its own. No ride was the same as any others, because of different group mates, different objectives, and different end products. After finishing each project, there's a feeling that "Hey, I did this!" that I can sort of get when I do well on something like a test, but not really. That's because my group and I had made something tangible, like a coffee table book or a film or board game. I feel satisfied knowing all the work that goes into something like that. Sure, it feels good when you ace a test, but that's just me feeling great about my grades. These projects make a person feel good about themselves.*

This is the sort of feedback that shows teachers they are on the right track and, like their students, need to keep persevering. Despite the natural ups and downs of implementing an innovative program, Patrice articulates what other Institute teachers feel—that this has been the hardest yet most satisfying work of their teaching careers and they are forever grateful for this opportunity.

Adriano Magnifico

M.Ed., P.Log. (professional logistics/supply chain designation), creator/adviser of the Career Internship Program, which began in 1995

- Career Internship Program (also known as CIP, pronounced "SIP")
- Current: Career and Entrepreneurship Consultant, Louis Riel School Division, Winnipeg, Canada
- 35 years as an English Language Arts/Advanced Placement teacher, Entrepreneurship and Business mentor
- Grades 9–12 main focus, but moving into junior high and elementary grades with entrepreneurship and career programming

This program was ahead of its time. Since 1995, CIP has promoted and implemented student-teacher partnership projects called "Tech Projects" with businesses, not-for-profit organizations, professional associations (such as the Canadian Manufacturers and Exporters), and other community partners based on mutual needs of students and partners. The projects run all year and are organized through English classes. Students build skills in other courses in the school (such as physics or chemistry) that aid in the planning and delivery of the Tech Projects. The projects inform a larger career mandate for students to help them identify their own skills, determine who values their skills outside high school walls, and connect with professionals to check out other skills they might like to acquire. The vast majority of CIP students show "focus" for a post high school plan.

Some examples of Tech Projects include the following:

- **Junior Achievement Projects**. Developed prototype, product, sales, and entrepreneurial verve (numerous projects—always smart to seek organizations that have infrastructure already in place).
- **Hovercraft Provincial Competition**. Built and purposed hovercraft sponsored by the Canadian Manufacturers and Exporters (numerous times).
- **Special Olympics Manitoba**. Organized opening ceremonies for Provincial Games.

- **Council on Drugs and Alcohol (CODA)**. Organized provincial marketing campaign.
- **Mood Disorders Association of Manitoba**. Facilitated mental health awareness project.
- **Alec's Scarves.** Created local school charity (named after student creator) that knitted scarves for needy children during winter months.
- **Winnipeg Cyclone Professional Basketball Team**. Planned and ran on-court marketing activities for fans and marketing team (entire season).
- **AHL Manitoba Moose Professional Hockey Team**. Created and implemented Inaugural Manitoba Moose Kids Club (entire season).
- **Western Glove Works**. Developed youth marketing survey on product lines, included presentation to Executive Board.
- **Manitoba Museum**. Proposed and planned museum summer activity that spanned entire province, presented before Board of Directors.
- **Children's Wish Foundation**. Planned and implemented world's largest toboggan run (204 people) with company *Movement by Design,* raised $18,000.

Skills involved in Tech Projects: Teamwork, entrepreneurship, project management, personal self-awareness, communication, digital, and media skill acquisition based on project need.

CIP opened up possibilities for students to apply their learning in real-life contexts and to pick up new skills and networks along the way. Previous academic programs lacked projects of this scope and magnitude with real audiences and were mostly teacher-led with most project work led by the perceived smart academic kids in the class. CIP projects are based on student interest, curiosity, skill needs, and collaborative potential with the community. The projects must address a real need by partners.

CIP is a yearlong program. An important innovation is that teachers use English class as the conduit through which all planning and organization flows. An English class in first semester begins the thinking, planning, and collaboration to build foundations for the Tech Project. A second semester English class moves from project planning to implementation in conjunction with partners from the community-at-large. The projects include outcomes that truly matter to outside audiences. Since 1995, students and teachers have completed about 350 Tech Projects.

CIP has spawned hybrid programs in four other high schools in the division that are designed to help students engage projects with real audiences and which fit the needs of their particular school cultures. The original CIP exists at Windsor Park Collegiate with 60 students. Hybrids exist at Nelson McIntyre Collegiate (32); J. H. Bruns Collegiate (35); Collège Jeanne Sauvé, a unique French Immersion iteration (25).

Teachers who lead their CIP programs include Carla Allan (Windsor Park), Angela Kaisser (J. H. Bruns), Ryan Sabourin (Nelson McIntyre). Adriano chairs a teacher-PLG with these teachers called the Innovation Group, which also includes other teachers in the division interested in pursuing more relevant and innovative classroom pedagogy.

Students in exit interviews and assessments rate their skills—digital, teamwork, self-awareness, project management, entrepreneurship, post-secondary focus, and others as 25–70% higher from September to June. Attendance in this PBL program is 10% higher than in other classes. Student averages in courses are overall higher than in their previous semesters without the program, a signal about the value of the making school as relevant as possible.

Assessments are a combination of overall course work from different courses, and the PBL project, a detailed interview with a unique device we've created call the "Career Canvas" that focuses on how school connects to life choices, the Tigers' Den Entrepreneurship events (another of our inventions) that gauges ideation and innovation skills, and a final June one-hour interdisciplinary presentation that synthesizes the year and probes this single question: What have I learned this year? The presentations are incredible. Students also are mentored by professionals outside school settings, and we share their feedback in exit interviews. Teachers include the Conference Board of Canada's *Innovation Skills Profile 2.0* to measure their skill development and innovative output.[32]

Using PBL as a focus for the past twenty-two years has earned CIP and its hybrids a dozen awards for innovative curriculum design, course delivery, and community partnership leadership. Adriano has been fortunate in that CIP has connected him to worlds beyond traditional classrooms, and highlighted that some of the best classrooms are in volunteer sites, professional workplaces, schoolyards, community clubs, senior centers, hockey rinks—anywhere students can build skills, foster relationships, seek mentorships, and discover personal truths as they explore post high school possibilities. The possibilities for PBL are endless if teachers open their minds to new classroom settings and community partners.

Cheap Advice for teachers: Dive in . . . do stuff that matters to students, include them in the creation, design, and assessment of assignments and activities, connect them to the community, and allow them a voice in their education. You will get powerful work from even the most average students when they feel they are truly investing in themselves. Good luck . . . oh, and it makes teaching way more fun and relevant to YOU.

Go to THEPBLPLAYBOOK.com for more resources, materials, and guiding questions about this chapter.

CHAPTER 19:

Building a Community of Lifelong Learners

XOXXOXOOXO

Ahh, IKEA.

If you are anything like me, you probably have a love/hate relationship with IKEA. I love walking through their store, putting our kids in childcare, and seeing all the possibilities (and cheap prices) of their furniture.

Even though their carts turn like they have a mind of their own, I still keep coming back and back again with my wife to get things for our house (and especially for our four kids' rooms).

Last week we headed to IKEA because my youngest was turning two years old, and she was asking for a "big girl" bed of her own!

Sure enough, IKEA had what we wanted, and we picked it out and loaded the four huge boxes into our car. The entire way home my thoughts were on how long this would take to put together. It was Saturday, and there was college football to watch, stuff to do around the house, and a party to get ready for the very next day.

I got myself all set up for some work time and unloaded all four boxes into her room. The parts were everywhere, but IKEA did a great job organizing them, color coding them, and giving me a clear set of directions on how to build the bed.

A few hours later my task was complete! I followed the steps, took my time, and voilà! We had a big-girl bed ready.

While I was putting the IKEA bed together and following the steps, I couldn't help but think that this is what many of our students must feel like.

They are often given "big tasks" to complete in school. These tasks could be writing a paper, research essay, book report project, word problem, or lab.

In each case, the task must seem like it is going to take forever for the learner to complete. But then, we break it down step-by-step. We give students the exact directions and models on how to finish the work. We outline a rubric and project guidelines that keep the student working at a good pace, and urge them to take it step-by-step until it is completed the "right" way.

While this might seem like a good thing, I'd argue it is one of the biggest issues we have in our education system right now.

It's hard to foster creativity and innovation when kids are always asked to follow the rules and complete the steps.

Here are four big takeaways I had from the IKEA experience and what our education system has in common:

1. IKEA is easy. But I didn't learn anything.

IKEA makes it easy to build a bed, a table, a chair, or anything else you might need in your house. I've personally built an entertainment unit, dresser with eight drawers, coffee table, two beds, desk, a couch, and two chairs from IKEA.

Yet I didn't learn anything. I can't even call it "building" because it was more like following the steps of a Lego set than learning how to create anything.

How many times do our kids finish and create something in school but not learn anything because they are following prescribed steps and guidelines?

2. IKEA is about compliance. Satisfaction is only in getting it done/finishing.

The only thing I got from the process is that I better really pay attention to the directions or along the way I'll mess up the product and have to go back and start all over again. If I was not compliant, I would be getting penalized because there was only ONE right way to make this bed.

After the bed was complete, I'll admit, I did feel a sense of satisfaction. However, it was in having a finished product that was good enough for my daughter to use. The more I thought about it, the more I realized the process had duped me into thinking I was making, but really I was just following. My self-worth was tied into how well I could follow directions, not how well I could make something.

3. IKEA is convenient. It's not creative.

You know what was great about this process from IKEA? It didn't take too much time. It was extremely convenient to drive to the store and pick out which item we wanted. Slide it into the back of the car. Bring it up to her room and have it finished in an hour or two.

It was extremely convenient.

But it wasn't creative. I remember giving students in my classroom a project where they had to design a website for one of the books we were reading. The only problem was I gave them the exact website builder to use. I told them which template to choose. I showed them an example that had the website laid out in a very specific way. I gave them a rubric which specified what content should be where on the website. I actually had points for how many pictures, video, and media items should be on the website. I shared three options for color palettes.

When my students turned in these websites, they all looked the same. Sure, they had made a website. But there wasn't anything creative about it. It was a convenient way for them to share information in a "cool" way. But they didn't learn much along the way.

4. IKEA is standardized. It is prime for hacking.

That night as I was talking to my wife about IKEA, I was searching online and found an entire website dedicated to hacking IKEA products. It turns out that people have actually been building and modifying IKEA products for a long time, but it has been an offshoot community of hackers:

> *IkeaHackers.net is a site about modifications on and repurposing of Ikea products. Hacks, as we call it here, may be as simple as adding an embellishment, some others may require power tools and lots of ingenuity.*
>
> *It was in May 2006 that I did a search on IKEA hacks and saw that there were so many amazing ideas floating on the Internet. How great it would be if I could find them all in one place, I thought.*
>
> *3 seconds later.*
>
> *A light bulb exploded in my brain and the rest, as they say, rolled out like Swedish meatballs. It took me a few nights of sleepless HTML-ing but I'm happy I did.*[33]

When something is as standardized and centralized as IKEA, it is prime for hacking. People come up with creative ideas on their own.

A standardized environment always has a group trying to break free of the constraints and make something better and powerful, whether it be IKEA or education.

This book is meant to be a reflection on what I saw in my own classroom, and what I see as something we all struggle with, in education. I had to ask the question:[34]

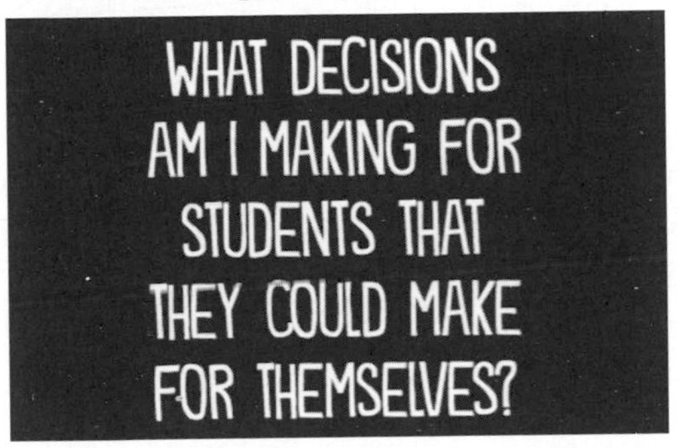

We want students to be successful, so we scaffold and build up support systems for them to find success. But where is the line? How can we support student success, celebrate them making mistakes along the way, and make time for them to learn during the process of creating, instead of just following a process to create?

One veteran teacher who has led the move to project-based learning said to me, ***"I keep thinking things might get easier. But they never do. I guess I'm hoping for the wrong thing. Instead, things are getting better for our kids. They are having new experiences we could never have offered 5, 10, 15 years ago. It's not easy for us, but it's the right thing to do."***

That last line stopped me cold. I had forgotten why we are here.

We aren't here for the new and shiny. Sure, the learning spaces, technology, and all kinds of updates are great.

But that's not what it is all about.

Innovation, as author George Couros says, **is new and better.**

But it does not matter if it is new and better unless it is better for our learners.

Over the past few months, I've been hit multiple times with the same truth: our work as educators REALLY matters. I've said that before to people, and I've heard it in classes and presentations . . . but for some reason I didn't put it all together until recently.

Do you remember watching those Coca-Cola commercials? The ones where one person did a small act of kindness and then it continued to spread throughout the day. Teaching is a lot like that, except the way we handle students in our classroom can blossom farther and wider than you may ever imagine.

Two recent events in my life made this so apparent.

I received an e-mail from a former student. He was reaching out to tell me about his college experience and what path he was headed down. I couldn't help but get emotional as I read his story. He hadn't been a "stand out" high school student, but he was always ready to be challenged in my class. And he didn't back down from anything I threw at him. He recently read Adam Braun's new book, *The Promise of a Pencil* (highly recommended!) and told me Adam's story had validated his idea that a life based around service was more valuable than a life based around money.

He is at a great college and chose to intern at a nonprofit instead of fight for a prestigious internship at a big Fortune 500 company. Is this a realistic path for every student? Probably not. But we need individuals who are ready to serve at a young age. He wrote about some different activities we had done in class like, Project: Global Inform and the Flat Classroom Project. Both had made him think outside the typical path. I realized what we do in our classrooms . . . can deeply affect our students and the world.

Students Changing the World Together

A school group that I cosponsor called "FANS" had presented to our school board. The two leaders of the club came right from lacrosse practice dressed in sweats (and a bit dirty) to an event where everyone else was dressed appropriately! They arrived a bit late but were full of passion. As we stepped up to the podium to speak, I explained that this club "FANS" had a main purpose of cheering and supporting all school activities and athletics. FANS was actually an acronym for "Following Activities N' Sports." Four years ago students in my class and Steve Mogg's class said the #1 thing they wanted to change about our school was the "culture." We started the FANS club with eight members . . . and four years later we have almost 500 members.

The school board was so proud of what our students had accomplished. They spoke about other schools asking them about the club, how we had been featured in local publications, and the *Huffington Post* . . . and talked about their own children at our school and why FANS mission was so important to include every student. At the end of the presentation, I realized we didn't even mention their volunteering at Special Olympics events each year . . . but it didn't matter, our students had shown adults that while the nation may focus on bullying—there is good going on at schools around the country and the world. There are students going out there and supporting each other for no other reason than because they care. I can only imagine how they will change the world.

What Is Our Role as Educators?

I've learned so much from students over the years, but the most important lesson I've taken away is that "they want to matter." Angela Maiers is so great at spreading this message, and so many other teachers, leaders, and educators have brought the "You Matter" mentality back into education.

Our role is to give students the opportunity to do work that matters. We need to give students choices and pathways that might not exist in our school yet. Here are five simple ways we can all change our classrooms so that students can change the world:

1. Give assignments and projects that include choice

If we don't give students choice, then it's difficult for them to break the traditional school barriers. Choice through inquiry-based assignments and projects is a real motivator and supercharges "change-making" ideas.

2. Spend time listening to what they want to change

You can't tell students they matter, and then not give them a say in the learning process. Each week make time to actually "talk" to your students about not only their lives but the school as well. What do they want to change?

3. Provide a forum for student-adult collaboration

Clubs are a great way for students and adults to work together. But break out of the traditional school "clubs" and make new clubs that have a purpose besides looking good on a transcript.

4. Don't limit their ideas

I've done this too often, and I try to catch myself. Let students' ideas speak for themselves. There needs to be a "Why" and a "How," but don't limit either with adult assumptions.

5. Share new stories

If you are sharing stories in class of people following only a traditional path, then students will think that's all there is in terms of success. Share new stories of people like Adam Braun . . . and watch their minds run wild with possibilities.

As a teacher and an adult, I need to be constantly reminded that what we do everyday matters to each individual student, the entire school, our communities, and the world. If you don't teach with that in the back of your mind, you are limiting the kind of impact you and your students can have.

Middle school Innovation class teacher, Jason Vest, told me this story about one of his students:

> *We had been working on a project that would take us to VCU (Virginia Commonwealth University) to present to a group of exchange students from China, two college professors, our principal, and the entire class. We were presenting Chindogu (useless, yet useful tool) where students had to actually design a tangible product and present it to the audience. One particular student's parent emailed me three times that morning saying their kid was beyond nervous and wasn't sure if they could go through with it. My principal even received an email and a phone call in regards to the same student! We both gave the student a pep talk and lo and behold, CRUSHED the presentation. Fast-forward two weeks later, that same student who was scared to death to utter a word was the only student in my Civics class that raised their hand to volunteer to run*

for "president" in our school-wide mock election. In PBL, students are able to challenge themselves. They are able to be creative and think outside the box, while becoming self-aware.

In PBL, there are always struggles. You struggle with breaking the fixed mind-set that students have been forced to comply with their whole time in schools. You struggle with reassuring students that it's not only okay to take risks, but encouraged. You struggle with getting students to see that they are truly being empowered to take control of their own lives by solving the real-world problems around them. Of course, these are the types of struggle that you dream of as a teacher. The wins for me have come in the form of student and parent anecdotes. "I love this class." "I like this class because it lets you be yourself." "We get to try and change the world in any way that you can." "Thank you for bringing out the creativity in my child again." This is the true power of PBL. When students are engaged in meaningful work, it doesn't seem like work at all. In fact, school becomes fun again.

Meaningful Learning

Last week I had the opportunity to take a group of students from our High School to the Franklin Institute. It was the first "road trip" for our Student Innovation Lab. About 20 students and 5 teachers/leaders made the trip where we learned about how the brain works, and why empathy is so important to any meaningful change process.

Our Student Innovation Lab gets kids from all walks of life together to solve real, meaningful problems at our school, going through the design-thinking process and getting opportunities like this one (at Franklin Institute, at UPenn, at Google NY, and other spaces like RecPhilly) to meet with experts and mentors in the field.

At lunch, we had a group of students who were still a bit hesitant on the whole process. One student said, "People are always trying to change, but nothing ever really changes."

I watched the conversation continue as the Chief Bioscientist and Chief Astronomer from the Franklin Institute sat down to have lunch with our students. The table became quiet. After introductions I pointed back to the conversation we had earlier about change and the Chief Bio-scientist asked our students, "Why do you think change is so hard?"

One of our kids piped up. "It just seems like **nothing changes if nothing changes.** Lots of people talk about changing something, or solving a problem, but most people won't do the work."

She smiled.

So did I.

Then she acknowledged our kids for taking a risk being here and working toward finding solutions to some of the biggest problems at our school. She said, "One thing you'll notice when trying to solve big problems is that we often try to do old things in new ways. For years we tried to improve travel by making better horseshoes, or better carriages, or better wheels for those carriages. Then someone has the idea that we don't need horses. We can use a machine to get us from place to place. That's a new thing in a new way. But even the car is not as revolutionary as a plane. People could imagine a car perhaps; they definitely could not imagine a plane. Flying was *impossible* until someone went out there and made it possible."

The conversation continued as our students got to talk shop with these amazing professionals for over an hour. But, that line stuck with me. **Are we trying to do old things in new ways, or are we looking to do new things in new ways?**

Whatever we do, let's do it together. Share out your story with the world, and have your students do the same. Whether your journey with PBL is just starting, or ready to ramp up, take this opportunity to remember why it matters: we all learn best through doing. Let's give our kids a chance to make, create, design, and do while they are in school, so when they leave our schools, they are ready to change the world.

Go to THEPBLPLAYBOOK.com for more resources, materials, and guiding questions about this chapter.

About A.J. Juliani

A.J. Juliani is the Director of Technology and Innovation at Centennial School District and a leading educator in the area of innovation, design thinking, and inquiry-based learning. Juliani has worked as a Middle and High School English Teacher, a K-12 Technology Staff Developer, and Education and Technology Innovation Specialist.

A.J. is the author of books centered around student-agency, choice, innovative learning and empowerment. As a parent of four young children, A.J. believes we must be intentional about innovation in order to create a better future of learning for all of our students. You can connect with A.J. on his blog, "Intentional Innovation" (located at ajjuliani .com) or through Twitter (@ajjuliani).

Bring A.J. Juliani to Your School or Event

A.J. Juliani brings a high-energy, fun, and engaging style of presentation through keynotes, full-day workshops, and online professional development offerings. His mix of personal stories from the classroom, real-world examples, and research based insights lead to a learning opportunity for everyone in attendance. A.J. has worked at all levels of the K-12 spectrum and has the lens of a parent as well. He will encourage educators to not only be intentional about innovation, but also focus on how our practice needs to always be centered on the student experience.

What People Are Saying About A.J. Juliani

"I was captivated by your presentation. Honestly, most keynote addresses usually don't hit home, but yours definitely got my brain working overtime."

"The best keynote I've been to in a long time. Thank you for sharing with us. I hope to be mindful of this inspirational feeling always."

"I really can't explain how awesome A.J. Juliani is! Inspiring, funny and more importantly, making me reflect on my practice."

Popular Messages From A.J. Juliani

Many of A.J.'s presentations are created specifically for your event, audience, and school. To get a sense of the topics A.J. presents on most, here are some previous keynote presentations he has done in the past:

- The Power of Project-Based Learning to Transform Your Classroom
- Empower: What Happens When Students Own Their Learning
- The Power of Inquiry and Choice: 20% Time and Genius Hour Projects
- Intentional Innovation: How to Guide Risk-Taking, Build Creative Capacity, and Lead Change
- Student-Centered Classrooms for Today's Student: Engaging All Learners Through Choice, Technology and Innovative Practices
- Technology With a Purpose: Empowering Students With Choice and Technology
- Design Thinking and the Maker Movement in K-12

Connect

Connect with A.J. Juliani for more information about bringing him to your event.

Email: ajjuliani@gmail.com
Twitter: @ajjuliani
Blog: ajjuliani.com

Endnotes

1. Jonathan C. Erwin, *The Classroom of Choice* (Alexandria, VA: Association for Supervision and Curriculum Development,1998), 68, 72, 66–67.

2. Eric Jensen, *Teaching with the Brain in Mind* (Alexandria, VA: Association for Supervision and Curriculum Development,1998), 66–67.

3. Article: https://blog.newsela.com/blog/2017/7/25/u2tlzoasa0gur7ua7uij7ihtop6dkp

4. Article: https://hbr.org/2010/06/column-you-are-what-you-measure

5. https://www.jaymctighe.com/wp-content/uploads/2011/04/Yes_but_objections_to_UbD1.pdf

6. http://dangerouslyirrelevant.org/2016/03/the-biggest-indictment-of-our-schools-is-not-their-failure-to-raise-test-scores.html

7. http://dangerouslyirrelevant.org/2016/03/the-biggest-indictment-of-our-schools-is-not-their-failure-to-raise-test-scores.html

8. Strobel & van Barneveld, 2009; Walker & Leary, 2009

9. National Clearinghouse for Comprehensive School Reform, 2004; Newmann & Wehlage, 1995

10. Condliffe et al., 2016

11. https://www.bie.org/object/document/research_summary_on_the_benefits_of_pbl

12. http://ajjuliani.com/genius-hour-is-enough/

13. https://medium.com/@thisissethsblog/no-laptops-in-the-lecture-hall-1847b6d3315

14. https://austinkleon.com/2018/01/11/good-theft-vs-bad-theft/

15. https://www.bie.org/about/what_pbl

16. https://rosscoops31.com/2017/10/22/pblplanningtemplate/

17. Frank, Anne, and Gerrold van der Stroom, *Anne Frank's Tales from the Secret Annex Including Her Unfinished Novel Cady's Life* (Random House Publishing Group, 2003).

18. https://signalvnoise.com/posts/3424-my-mother-made-me-a-scientist-without-ever

19. http://ajjuliani.com/inquiry-its-not-a-new-idea-launchbook/

20. https://www.sciencedirect.com/science/article/pii/S0010027712001849?via%3Dihub

21. https://www.youtube.com/watch?v=8lGjOtIQ1YQ

22. https://www.youtube.com/watch?v=1gat0diHi80

23. https://youtu.be/lrXyBlxhVq4; https://youtu.be/uHkmE4XoEZ4; https://youtu.be/EPfsiRwCs3; https://youtu.be/cFD8Uv1urTk

24. https://docs.google.com/spreadsheets/d/1Tw-mLtorFnn8JlBalu6HzOsT-vwbVFWvumA5vAsfnrs/edit?usp=sharing

25. https://docs.google.com/presentation/d/1vwehieBt6BEWfY-SMHHEP_r0KL3DE55kMIT7h4bjwiY/edit?usp=sharing

26. https://genius.com/Robert-greene-mastery-introduction-annotated

27. https://www.glyndewis.com/an-old-man-a-boy-and-a-donkey/?v=7516fd43adaa

28. https://georgecouros.ca/blog/archives/5090

29. http://www.senseandsensation.com/2013/05/manifesto-art-and-science-of-education.html

30. http://www.senseandsensation.com/2013/05/manifesto-art-and-science-of-education.html

31. https://www.huffingtonpost.com/katherine-von-jan/unstructured-classroom_b_1024404.html

32. http://www.conferenceboard.ca/docs/default-source/public-pdfs/InnovationSkillsProfile.pdf?sfvrsn=0

33. https://www.ikeahackers.net/about

34. Visual by John Spencer in *Empower: What Happens When Students Own Their Learning*